Taking Charge of Your Child's Education

A guide to becoming the primary influence in your child's life.

ERICA ARNDT

Taking Charge of Your Child's Education

By Erica Arndt

Book, Cover Design & Graphics by: Erica Made Designs, LLC

ISBN: 978-0-9861160-0-1

Additional works by this author are available at www.confessionsofahomeschooler.com
Printed in the United States of America.

This book is dedicated to all of the beloved
parents who have committed their lives to
raising their children with purpose.

Thank you!

To God for His many blessings and for His continued faithfulness in my life. To my family for all of their support and encouragement. To all of my loyal readers without whom this book would not be possible. I hope it blesses you and your family!

And a special thank you to my mom and editor, for a lifetime of support, and for taking the time to read every last word.

Disclaimer:

I am not a legal attorney, nor do I have a degree in law.
The information contained in this book is what I have gleaned from my own research and should not be taken as legal advice.

This book may contain affiliate links from which I benefit directly.

Table of Contents

1

About Me

"Commit to the Lord whatever you do, and he will establish your plans. ~ Proverbs 16:3

It was twelve years ago that our lives completely changed. People often ask me if it was hard each time we had a new baby. But really it was when we had our first child that things got crazy.

When you go from zero to one child, everything changes. We were used to doing whatever we wanted, whenever we wanted. We didn't have to work around feedings or naptimes. We could go to dinner at 10pm if we wanted to!

Of course, when we had our first child, it was love at first sight. The thought of dropping her off at a daycare seemed inconceivable. So we decided that I would leave my professional career path and become a stay at home mom.

I was a manager in a fast growing Information Technologies company. And boy was it an adjustment coming home from the professional world. I went from a world full of adult interaction, I enjoyed lunch with friends, had a job where I felt appreciated, one where I felt validated. Looking back now, I realize that my job defined me. My work was who I was.

Suddenly I found myself home alone with a baby.

My professional friends moved on, and I found myself slightly out of my comfort zone. Now I entered into in a position where my daily accomplishments included changing diapers, feeding my baby, doing laundry, cleaning the house, and if my husband was lucky, making a homemade meal for dinner.

I loved it, and hated it, all at the same time. I loved my baby, I loved taking care of her, but I missed conversing with other adults. I missed feeling like I was actually accomplishing something important. Dishes, diapers, laundry, and cooking just weren't that rewarding of a career for me. I don't know about you, but I really hated that giant purple singing dinosaur!

To say that I was overwhelmed was an understatement. How could we possibly handle all of this new found responsibility? Worse yet, what if we made the wrong choice and scarred our children for life?

We were drowning in diapers, mealtimes, bedtimes, bath times, and playtimes, oh my! I wasn't even thinking about college, let alone elementary school! I was merely trying to get through each day as it came! Honestly, the thought of picking out schools and worrying about the future education of another person, wasn't exactly on my radar.

Over the course of just a few years God blessed us with three more wonderful children. And not long afterwards their futures quickly became a top priority!

How would we make sure they received the best education? How would we prepare our children for their futures?

All of those questions from well-meaning friends and family started rolling in.

"Where will they go to school?"

"I heard this one is the best.

"You better enroll now so you can hope to get a spot in the next 5 years."

"Our children went here, it only costs a zillion dollars for preschool, but it's worth it!"

"Don't delay; you'll never get into the preschool of your choice if you do!"

Like all good parents, we taught our children how to do things on their own, of course. We taught them to feed themselves, dress themselves, and how to do basic day-to-day tasks appropriate for their age levels.

As the years passed, we began to feel the calling of homeschooling on our family. We had several long discussions regarding education. What we thought was best, what we thought other people wanted us to do, and what we felt God was calling us to do.

Eventually we took a leap of faith, decided not to let the fear of what others would say influence us, and decided to try homeschooling.

For those of you who don't know much about me, my name is Erica. I'm a Christian, a wife, a mom to four wonderful children, and a reluctant homeschooler.

Yes, a very reluctant homeschooler.

A few of those callings were a surprise to me at first. My Christian testimony is a long one, so I'll spare you the details. But let's just say that God swooped in just in time to save my marriage, my soul, and I've been a changed person ever since.

The mom part wasn't too much of a surprise; I hoped maybe someday I'd have one or two children. But having four of these little darlings was definitely a surprise! Of course, it has turned out to be a blessed one.

Our homeschooling decision was probably the biggest surprise of them all. In fact prior to our decision to homeschool I believe the words "I will never…", actually came out of my mouth. I was adamantly opposed to homeschooling, and quite frankly thought it a disservice to our children to go that route.

After having two of our four children, God began to slowly change my heart. Reluctantly, we started homeschooling our oldest when she was ready to start preschool.

Each year I relied on my backup plan of putting her in school if things went south. It's what made me feel like I could give homeschooling a go. I mean, if we failed we could just put her in school and move on, no harm, no foul, right?

As they say, time flies! Now, nine years later, we are still going strong and are finally confident in our decision for our children's education. Over the past several years I've come to embrace the fact that I am not in control. I'm not a super mom with all of the answers. I don't have it "all together", so to speak.

And contrary to common stereotypes, I do not have an overabundance of patience! As a matter of fact, I'm probably one of the least patient people I know. But God is in control of my life, and for that I am eternally grateful. I'm just like you, a parent who wants to do the best for my children.

So it is from deep within a mom's heart that I write this book. My hope is that it will inspire you to take an active role in your child's life now, and continue on in the future.

The Professionals

"And these words which I command you today shall be in your heart. You shall teach them diligently to your children, and shall talk of them when you sit in your house, when you walk by the way, when you lie down, and when you rise up. You shall bind them as a sign on your hand, and they shall be as frontlets between your eyes. You shall write them on the doorposts of your house and on your gates. - Deuteronomy 6:6-7

So why take charge of your child's education? Why not leave their education to the professionals? If you read the verse above, you'll see that God has placed the responsibility of raising our children upon us as parents.

Even with the best of our intentions, one of the things affecting our families today is a higher level of government control over our children's education. States are more strictly dictating what curriculum and courses schools and teachers are allowed to offer.

Many are tied to teaching students simply to perform well on standardized testing. Unfortunately the mandate to teach the same materials to all students not only puts a damper on teacher creativity, but also on the student's ability to learn said materials. Gone are the days of elective classes and school being something that is enjoyable. Instead we've entered into an era of statistics and rankings, often sacrificing our previous personal approach to teaching.

If you have a student in a public or private school system, then you are already familiar with these requirements. There is probably not much leeway for individual interests or customization for your child's education without paying a high price for private schooling.

But I want to encourage you that no matter which educational choices you make for your family, it doesn't mean that you can't still be the primary influence on your child's life and their learning.

If you've chosen public education, your choices might be limited, but you can still have significant impact upon your child's life.

If you homeschool, you probably still have a bit of freedom in choosing curriculum depending on what state you live in. However new regulations to control educational materials are quickly coming our way.

The only way to remain in charge of our child's development is to take an active stance, and to parent with a purpose. How we choose to raise our children is something that is personal to each individual family.

Though we have chosen to educate our children at home, this book isn't about selling you on homeschooling. It's about encouraging you to take charge of your child's future. It is about creating a legacy that will carry down onto future generations to come.

Whatever educational decisions your family has made, you as a parent have the freedom and capability to take charge and be more involved in your child's life.

Taking charge of your child's education isn't just about academics.

Taking charge of your child's education isn't just about academics. There are so many educational options these days, and honestly we were overwhelmed with all of the choices.

But after 12 years, we finally figured out that the real lessons that will influence our children most aren't in the method of schooling we chose, but instead they originate right here in our own home.

As you read through this book, you'll notice sections titled "Taking Charge". These sections are full of helpful tips and ideas to help you take charge in various areas of your own home. I hope you find them useful, and that they will encourage you in your parenting journey.

3

Parenting is Not a Spectator Sport

"For we are His workmanship, created in Christ Jesus for good works, which God prepared beforehand, that we should walk in them." - Ephesians 2:10

Chances are if you're reading this book you have a vested interest in creating the best environment possible to foster your child's education and future as they move into adulthood.

In this increasingly competitive environment, your child's education should be a growing area of importance. As parents our number one desire is for our children to mature into successful adults. Although the term "success" can differ from person to person, it all starts with the basic educational process for our children.

And by education, I don't simply mean the three R's; reading, writing, and arithmetic. Although those are certainly helpful, the education of your child is so much more than that.

The dictionary defines education as the "process of receiving or giving systematic instruction at a school or university." But I challenge you to not only think of your child's education solely as academics. Instead consider it the process of imparting reasoning, judgment, life skills, character, morals, values, and ethics for future generations to come.

After all, how many of us would be comfortable with our child growing into a brain surgeon with absolutely zero work ethic, morals, or compassion for their patients?

Raising our next generation is not a part-time job, nor is it something you do only when you have the time. As parents, we are on call 24/7 and it is our God given responsibility to be an active participant in the lives of our children.

Unfortunately, children don't exactly come with an owner's manual, no matter how much we wish they did! But God did provide us with direction and guidance, to help us through our parenting journey. But we'll discuss more about that as we proceed.

As you read through this book, I think you'll find a common theme of getting and staying involved in all aspects of your child's life. If we truly want to take charge of our child's education, we need to think outside of the "academic" box and come to the realization that their education begins in our own home.

For now, that is still an area where we have control. We set the mood, atmosphere, and overall environment of our own homes. It can be a cold, critical place to be. Or it can be a loving, encouraging, and welcoming place to be. That is up to us. My hope is that this book encourages you to make well informed decisions regarding your child's future, and begin parenting with a purpose and goal in mind.

Taking Action

Commit today to parenting with purpose! Commit your time, your energy, and your life to not only raising your child, but to living your life as a testimony they can follow.

Determine to leave a legacy for your children. Strive to show them what it is like to grow up in a home where they are valued, encouraged, and loved.

4

Be their Primary Influence

"Behold, children are a heritage from the Lord, the fruit of the womb a reward." - Psalms 127:3

Sadly one of the main shifts in today's society is the absence of parental influence in the home. Many parents have stepped back and allowed teachers, coaches, student peers, and others to become the primary influence in their child's life and education.

It is a common misconception that others, the "professionals", are a better influence then we are when it comes to raising our children. But that's not entirely true.

As a parent your child naturally looks to you for support, encouragement, and to teach them basic morals of right and wrong. All research shows that parental involvement in a child's learning is an invaluable factor in improving that child's academic and social achievements.

Whether your child is in a school system or being educated at home, as their parent you have the opportunity to create a good quality home environment where children feel welcomed, supported, loved, and encouraged.

While it is certainly acceptable for students to have proper role models in their lives in the form of teachers, coaches, and other adult influences, the primary influence should still be from you, their parent. Creating an environment of acceptance in your home is a great way to encourage your children to seek you first when dealing with life issues they may face.

One of the best ways to create a sense of connection with your child is to be available to them. Spend time with your child, listen to them, play games together, and stay up to date on their day-to-day progress. By doing this consistently you will find that your parent-child relationship will, in turn, grow. And the likelihood that they will turn to you for guidance increases.

Children don't need more "stuff", they need more of our presence.

As we nurture our relationship with our children, we create an environment where learning can now take place. We will gain their trust, and they will in turn, start to respect us and our opinions. One of the most common things I hear from parents is that their children don't respect their parent's opinions as much anymore. You'll start hearing things like, "Well that's not what my teacher said." Somehow their teacher's opinions have become more valuable to them.

Fostering a good relationship with your child is the primary step to taking charge of their education. If you have a good connection with them, instead of arguing with you, they'll come home and tell you what they heard today and want to know what your opinion is on the matter.

As you read through this book, you'll find "taking action" areas at the end of the chapters. I really wanted to include some tangible things that will help give ideas of how you can purposefully enrich your relationship with your child and your family.

Below you'll find some suggestions to help begin fostering a positive relationship with your child, and your family as a whole.

Taking Action

- Read the Word together daily (i.e. Family devotion time).
- Set aside a little bit of one-on-one time for each of your children every day.
- Give your child your unconditional support, even when they make mistakes.

- Help your child learn from their mistakes in a constructive, non-criticizing way.
- Encourage your child in their interests.
- Create a loving and accepting environment, where your child can feel free to talk openly with you.
- Have fun with your child! Play games, read together, enjoy life together.
- Encourage family meal time at least once per day where you can talk and share.
- Talk and pray with your child before bedtime each day.

5

Education Isn't Just About Academics

"Train up a child in the way he should go; even when he is old he will not depart from it." - Proverbs 22:6

Often the term "education" evokes images of math drills, text books, worksheets, reading, and other various school related subjects. But as parents the term "education" not only includes academics, but it also includes many other facets of your child's developmental process. We do not want to rely solely on others to teach our children things like spiritual development, character traits, morals, values, life skills, and even academics. Through daily interaction with your child you can help teach them to analyze and comprehend the world around them.

Daily, parents are presented with multiple opportunities for spiritual, character, academic, social, and spending quality time with our children, if we are open to them. It's very easy to get caught up in the business of this world, running from one activity to the next, and for many, working too much.

Even as a homeschooling family, it is easy to get caught up in the daily routine of running around, and we can forget to actually spend time together.

One of our most precious commodities is time. More specifically time spent together as a family. And frankly speaking, that's really what our kids want from us. Time is increasingly important in today's world where the notion of more and more "stuff" is becoming a common addiction. I don't know about you, but my kids seem to want everything they see on TV, or at a friend's house. But all of that "stuff" doesn't fill our souls. It doesn't bless our family. As a matter of fact, we've found that the more "stuff" we accumulate, the less time we spend together. Kids tend to go off on their own rather than playing together and spending time with the family.

It breaks my heart when I hear parents say they can't wait for school to start again. I know kids get bored over breaks, but the sentiment is that their kids are a burden on their time. Instead I encourage them to spend time with their children doing something they enjoy. Learn to have fun with them, and relate to them on their level. And suddenly you're enjoying the time together as well!

These comments also remind me how quickly time passes, and how few years, we really have our children with us before they move on to live their own lives. If the average person lives, say 85 years, then the 18 years our kids spend with us is less than 1/4 of our lives. I don't ever want to look back and regret not taking advantage of each day with my children.

If you ever speak with someone in hospice, or the elderly, they'll tell you that the relationships we've had are what's important. You don't get to take the "stuff" with you when you go, but you do leave behind memories. You share your soul with those around you, and that is what gets passed on from generation to generation.

Today I want to encourage you to enjoy the time you have with your children now. None of us are guaranteed tomorrow, but we can embrace today!

Taking Action

Here are some practical things to consider when we're talking about your child's education. This is not an exhaustive list, but hopefully it will help you get started in the right direction. As you can tell by now, raising children takes more than just your time; it takes your heart as well.

Spiritual

Your children will naturally follow your lead while still younger. But it is up to us to help our children build their faith so that one day it becomes their own. You can help nurture their spiritual growth while in your home, and one of the best ways to do that is to practice what you preach. I know sometimes that is easier said than done, but keep in mind your children don't expect you to be perfect. Be real with them. Discuss with them some of your struggles, and how God has helped you through them. Let your faith be a living example of Christ. Even if it seems like they aren't listening to your words, they will be watching your actions.

The first step to accomplishing this is to have a solid walk with God yourself. Then let that overflow into your children. The second step is to be present. Spend time with them, and be available to them when they need you. Don't be tempted to push children off until you're done reading your email, or whatever thing that might be keeping your attention. Show your children they are important, making time for them will speak volumes!

Emotional

As your children grow up, their emotions will fluctuate quite a bit. From the toddler melt downs to the teen hormones, our children need to feel a sense of security when at home. Being accessible to them, and helping them work through their emotions in a constructive way is a very important aspect of your child's educational growth.

Make sure that you are always there to encourage your children. Let them know that they aren't facing trials on their own, but you and God are there to help them get through each aspect of life. As a parent, it should be boring how reliable that you are! With all of the difficulties our children face in today's world, knowing that you are always readily available to them will be paramount in their lives.

Life Skills

It is not often that our goal is to work ourselves out of a job. But as parents that's exactly what we are doing.

We are raising our children with the goal of sending them out on their own. In order for them to be successful they need to have basic skills to support themselves. This can range from developing shopping lists, cooking, cleaning, and doing laundry. But even more so, they also need to be able to make wise decisions when out on their own.

While they are in your home, take advantage of this time to teach them daily basics of managing their own home, teach them good decision making, life skills, and smart financial choices. Seize the time while you have it. The opportunity to impart your wisdom will be gone before you can blink, and if your children don't learn these lessons from you they'll struggle later in life.

Character

Having good character traits is a big deal in today's world. However, establishing good character isn't something that can be acquired in a short period of time. It's something that you will be developing in your children for years to come. It starts at the very beginning as you teach them to share their toys and how to handle their emotions in a better way than their natural urge to lash out in a temper tantrum.

Things like honesty, compassion, kindness, self-control, patience, and the like are all things that will need to be nurtured. While our children are still young we have the unique opportunity to teach them how to handle things more effectively. We can show them how to make good choices, and how to treat others as well.

I have a whole set of free character studies you're welcome to use. They can be found on my website under the printables, then Bible tab.

Ethics/Moral Values

As you consider passing down your ethical and moral values to your children, now is a good time to assess whether or not you yourself are a living example. We are all born selfish. It's just a fact. We naturally look out for ourselves first.

But that said, it's still up to us to pass on our moral values to our children, and show them how to honor and respect others as well. Teach them about teamwork, honoring others above themselves, serving others, kindness, gentleness, and compassion.

"Be devoted to one another in love Honor one another above yourselves." - Romans 12:10

Service

A great way to teach your children about serving others is through various volunteering projects. Have them volunteer at homeless shelters, animal shelters, or other philanthropy projects in your community.

This doesn't always have to be something big, you can start small by delivering a meal to a sick friend, making a nice card for a friend, or helping out someone else in need.

Whenever we go to the zoo, I always bring an extra lunch with us. Inevitably we come across people asking for money on the street corners. I don't always like to offer money, but I'm more than willing to offer them something to eat. *It might be the Italian in me coming out.*

I never thought my kids noticed, but now when we're making lunches for a field trip, my children always remind me to make an extra one in case we find someone along the way who needs it.

Another thing we like to do is shovel snow for the neighbors. One of our neighbors is an older lady whose husband is often away on business. My husband

and son often help her out by shoveling her driveway. She is always blessed by their kindness, and if you pay attention, you won't have to look far to find small things you can do to bless others.

At the same time you are showing your children how to care for others just as God has called us to do.

Responsibility

With a family of 6, teaching our children responsibility was a necessity. Without teamwork our home would be a disaster. But really I think it's important for any size family. Creating an environment where the entire family pitches in to keep the home running smoothly is an essential part of creating a functional home.

Along with preventing the entire load that comes with running a household from falling onto one person, you're also creating an atmosphere of teamwork. You're helping teach your children some very valuable life skills that will serve them well into adulthood.

We have a chore chart so everyone knows what is expected of them on any given day. I also try to divide out the tasks so they are even. Everyone chips in and helps out. Promoting an atmosphere where the whole family is working as a team also shows your children that they are a valued part of the family. It creates a place for them, and they receive satisfaction from contributing to the home.

It will also show them how to care for others, and how to become a good steward over what God has blessed them with. It also helps them gain a sense of worth and belonging to the family unit. We'll discuss this more in the chapter on teaching responsibility later on in this book.

6

Parenting is a Ministry

"And how from infancy you have known the Holy Scriptures, which are able to make you wise for salvation through faith in Christ Jesus. All Scripture is God-breathed and is useful for teaching, rebuking, correcting and training in righteousness, so that the man of God may be thoroughly equipped for every good work." ~ 2 Timothy 3:15-17

Many of us may think of a minister as a pastor. But when it comes down to it, you are a minister to your own family. If you can't tell by now, our journey starts with you!

Let's make sure we're all on the same page here. A minister is defined as "One who acts under the orders of another or who is employed by another to execute his purposes."

So who is our employer?

Whose orders are we acting under?

Really there are only two choices here. We can live by our own rules, or by God's. Once we recognize that God has blessed us with these children and has given us the tools needed to complete the task at hand, the whole prospect is not so overwhelming.

We are called as parents to minister to our children on a 24/7 basis. If it helps we can consider them as disciples. As a parent we can be challenged from all kinds of external and internal sources. We can doubt ourselves, compare ourselves and our children to others, get discouraged by daily trials, and we can face criticism from family and friends. Unfortunately, if we are not careful we can pass that discouragement on to our children as well.

Think about Christ and His disciples. The disciples were continually whining, complaining, and arguing over who was better. Sound familiar? If your house is anything like mine, that describes it to a tee! What was Jesus' response to his disciples? Did He lose his temper and yell at them? No, He patiently explained, over and over and over again. He was training them, ministering to them, and encouraging them based on God's Word. He also explained that whoever wanted to be first among them, had to indeed be last (Mark 10:44). I love that verse and use it often in our home!

God has placed these children in our care, not someone else's. He has given them to us to train up in righteousness. No matter how many times we may fail, lose our temper and yell, or be inconsistent in our discipline, we can rest in the fact that God knows us!

He did not make a mistake in giving these kids to us. He knows our strengths, weaknesses, and that we cannot raise our children without Him. We will fail if we are striving to complete this task in our flesh. Instead we need to learn to trust in God, and to lean on and seek Him for guidance, support and strength.

Dear friend if you haven't been dependent upon God before now, parenting will kick you right over to the other side where you will literally realize you can do nothing apart from Him!

As John 15:5 tells us "I am the vine; you are the branches. If you remain in me and I in you, you will bear much fruit; apart from me you can do nothing."

Here is the blessing received for our abiding in Christ… "I can do all things through Christ who strengthens me." ~ Philippians 4:13

If we can change our viewpoint and learn to see our parenting as a ministry to our family, that will change our perspective. It's not a daily burden, or a chore we need to complete before we can check our email. It is a ministry of love!

Ladies and gentlemen, we have the blessed honor of training up our children in righteousness no matter what type of schooling we have chosen.

Simply gaining a new perspective will help you see challenges as opportunities. For example your child's bad attitude during their math homework is actually a wonderful opportunity for us to teach them about perseverance!

But…before we can carry out God's love and vision for our family, I think it's important to remember who we are in God's eyes and what our real purpose is in raising our children. As a minister to your family, what is God's plan for you as a parent? Take some time today to remind yourself who you are in Christ.

I have a chart I want to share with you that I've referred to often over the years. It's primarily geared towards a mother however the principles can be applied to all parents.

Taking Action

Take some time to reflect on the parenting chart on the following page to see which side you currently fall on. If it's not the side you want to be on, pray over the areas you need to address, and make changes now.

There is a much lovelier and printable version on my website if you're so inclined to hang it on the fridge!

(http://www.confessionsofahomeschooler.com/blog/2010/02/super-mom-vs-abiding-mom.html)

Super Mom vs. Abiding Mom

Does	Is (Psalm 46:10)
Tries to impress others	Pleases the Lord (Eph. 5:10, Proverbs 29:25)
Is controlled by an agenda (curriculum, schedule, etc)	Is controlled by the Holy Spirit: (Gal. 5:22-26) (Uses curriculum & schedules as tools for orderliness so she's more free to follow the spirit)
Her self worth is found in her accomplishments (clean house, perfect kids, the perfect bulletin boards, etc.)	Her self worth is found in an accurate view of who she is in Christ Jesus (Eph 2:10)
Her peace is found in the "perfect" environment	Her peace is found in Jesus in the midst of any storm (Is 26:3)
She is discouraged by failure	Failure reminds her that God's strength is made perfect in weakness (2 Cor. 12:9-10)
She expects perfection from herself and others	She practices grace with herself and others. (Eph 4:32)
She teaches her kids to be good	She teaches her kids to be Godly (Proverbs 22:6)
She is frustrated with her lack of spiritual fruit	She abides in Christ and bears much fruit (John 15:5)
She does things with her children	She builds a relationship with her children (Deut 6:6-7)
Her perspective is based on what is seen	Her perspective is based on what is unseen (Col 3:2)
She chooses quantity of activities	She chooses the most excellent Way (I Cor 13)

Parenting is Love

"Love is patient, love is kind. It does not envy, it does not boast, it is not proud. It does not dishonor others, it is not self-seeking, it is not easily angered, it keeps no record of wrongs. Love does not delight in evil but rejoices with the truth. It always protects, always trusts, always hopes, always perseveres. Love never fails." - 1 Corinthians 13:4-8a

One of the most valuable things we can do to foster a positive upbringing for our children is simply to love them. If we are to have any influence on their successful journey towards adulthood we need to have a good relationship with our children. The best way to create that bond is to spend time with them, encourage them, and help them through whatever life throws their way.

For me, one of the most convicting passages in the Bible 1 Corinthians 13. Let's take a look at this passage in relation to our calling as parents.

1. Love is Patient

In a nutshell, love is not impatient. Let's just stop right here and ask ourselves a few questions...

"Am I ever impatient with my children?"

"Am I constantly rushing them so I can get onto other things?"

"Am I easily frustrated with them?"

Let's think back to our new perspective of parenting as a ministry and remember that we are training God's children. Our children cannot be held responsible for telling us how to raise them. Some children do great with regular schooling, others need more special attention. Some might require "out of the box" thinking in order to break open that mind of theirs and it's our job to find the right key to unlock it!

Love is...

Every time we're about to react in a less than edifying manner, try to remember that your child is probably just as frustrated as we are. They are looking to us for support and encouragement, and it is our responsibility to patiently teach them how to respond to life's challenges.

Think about it this way, how would you feel if your laptop was broken and the geek squad looked at you and said "Sorry lady, I can't help you!" You would feel lost, and probably helpless, maybe even hopeless!

Let's not leave our children hanging without a safety net. Make sure they know that you're there to catch them when they fall. Be a constant support to them, and help them find a way to persevere through the trials of life.

2. Love is kind

How often do you praise your children?

Do you let your emotions dictate how the day goes?

Our children are a training ground just begging for guidance. In Proverbs 15:1 we know that *"A gentle answer turns away wrath, but a harsh word stirs up anger."* Let's take the theory that you win more flies with honey than with vinegar, and apply that to our attitude towards our children. Are we blessing and encouraging our children through praise or are we exasperating them with harsh words and condemnation?

3. Love does not envy

Are you using your children's gifts and talents to bless and encourage them? Or are you frequently pointing out the negative and bad things that they do?

Are you allowing their disobedience to cause resentment in your feelings towards them?

The definition of envy is discontentment and resentment. If we envy other families over our own, we can begin to start to resent our spouse and children. As adults it is easy to continue to be angry with our children's disobedience long after the issue has occurred. Reflecting the grace we ourselves have been given, let's try to extend that to our children.

Deal with the issue immediately and move on, don't let bitterness and resentment creep in and steal away the precious time we have with our children!

4. Love does not boast

"When I was your age I had to walk to school in the snow…and it was up hill both ways!" ~ said every parent, ever.

We probably laugh about this age old story but it can actually cause issues in how our kids relate to us. Our children often don't understand sarcasm, nor are these stories most likely true. The only reason we are directed to say things like this is in attempt to belittle the issues they may be facing. Compassion for their immediate situation can be a much more effective teaching tool than boasting on how much you *may* have accomplished at their age.

Instead of relating to your children on a sarcastic level, take the time to speak words of kindness into their hearts. As they grow you'll find that they react to others in this same manner. It is much more rewarding to hear your child have compassion on another person than to react to them with cynicism.

And yes, I'm guilty of sharing the uphill both way story with my children too, but I added that I was surely barefoot!

5. Love is not proud

"Do I try to command obedience through fear and threat?"

"Do I give my children the impression that I never fail?"

God wants us to encourage our children, to let them know they are part of a family team. If they constantly feel inferior to us, then they will be crushed in spirit, and I don't want to be responsible for that. I try to be diligent and if necessary apologize when I've acted sinfully. Letting them know that Mom is not perfect, and that I too need to seek God for wisdom.

I try to let my kids know that it is our desire to teach them to learn each skill to mastery, and to succeed or at least try diligently, in all they do. I do not give grades for the most part. My hope is that my children will have the chance to master a subject before moving them on. We take our time, learn at their pace. As a schedule driven type person it is easy for me to let my curriculum dictate what I do on a daily basis. While I do try to keep to that, I've learned over the years that it's important to take the time to make sure my children are actually "learning and retaining" the information instead of rushing through something, just so we can stay on track with our lesson plan.

Within our home we work together as a family unit. Not one of them is more important than the other, but we stand together in unity. If someone is having a hard time learning something, we may stop everyone and do what we can as a team to help them get it.

I think this is one reason that the Chore Chart can be such an effective household tool. We work as a team to keep our house in order, and then we have time as a family to play and have fun!

6. Love does not dishonor others

Love does not behave rudely or act in an unbecoming order. A common mistake we make is to expose our children's sinful behavior to others. Many times I'll catch myself on the phone with a friend venting about how horrible our day was, including bad attitudes and learning issues we've had.

While you may think your children are not listening, I assure you they are. That kind of exposure can be very hurtful to our children. Please be careful to consider what's coming out of your mouth at all times. Our children need to know that we have their backs, and that they can trust and depend on us. Think of how you would feel if you heard your child telling their friends how mom yells all the time!

"Let no corrupt word proceed out of your mouth, but what is good for necessary edification, that it may impart grace to the hearers." ~Ephesians 4:29

7. Love is not self-seeking

Raising and disciplining our children is not an easy task. As a mom I know I tend to place my own expectations on my children. If you haven't noticed our children are all different from each other and from us! But let us remember that they have been fearfully and wonderfully made. (Psalm 139:14) God knew them before He formed them in our womb; before they were born they were set apart. (Jeremiah 1:5)

God did not make a mistake, He has created them perfect in His eyes. While their interests may not be the same as our interests, we need to respect and help them pursue their desires. Each of our children has different interests. Find out what that is, then actually take the time to spend some quality one on one time with your children doing things they like to do. It's not about us, it's about them! And what they want is our time, not our words.

8. Love is not easily angered

Oh this one hits home hard for me. I never realized I could fly off the handle so quickly until I had kids. I used to be calm, relaxed, and easy going. But boy can those little guys push my buttons!

Unfortunately, if I haven't started my day in fervent prayer seeking God for patience, I'll lose it in about 2 seconds. I did a search on "slow to anger" for this section. I found this...

"So then my beloved brethren, let every man be swift to hear, slow to speak, slow to wrath". ~ James 1:19

I also found a whole page of verses that came back stating that the Lord is slow to anger and abounding in love. Wow! I've been on the receiving end of His rich love so many times, why is it so hard for me to pour out that same love on my children? Let's be careful to be slow to anger and quick to listen to our children!

One of the verses I have memorized over the years is James 1:20 "For the wrath of man [mom] does not produce the righteousness of God." Yikes. I've read this verse many times, it's imprinted in my heart. And God is gracious to bring it back to memory whenever I'm on the edge of wrath.

9. Love keeps no record of wrongs

Ugh...another one for me! I have to say that I'm wonderful at remembering all the wrong things my children and husband have done over the years. I can recall in an instant that time several years ago when so-and-so did such-and-such. *Strangely though, I can't seem to remember what we ate for lunch yesterday without looking at my meal plan...hmm...*

But love keeps no record of wrongs! It's so easy to bring up some previous instance and beat our kids over the head with it when some opportunity for fun comes up.

"Mom, can I have a play date?"

"No! Remember yesterday when you did (fill in the blank here)!"

While I certainly believe it is important to use our children's poor choices as a teaching opportunity, be careful not to let these instances turn into bitterness in your own heart. Once something is resolved move forward, forgiving them just as your Father in heaven has forgiven you.

"Pursue peace with all people, and holiness, without which no one will see the Lord: looking carefully lest anyone fall short of the grace of God; lest any root of bitterness springing up cause trouble, and by this many become defiled." -Hebrews 12:14-15

Yikes, I do not want to be the one responsible for defiling anyone!

My beloved friends, do not let the root of bitterness rob you and your children from loving one another! Un-forgiveness is like a poison the offended party eats in hopes of causing pain to another, but in reality it will eat us up!

How many times should we forgive each other? Matthew 18:22 tells us seventy seven times. Some translations say seventy times seven. Either way, I think the point is to forgive as many times as it takes.

How many times has your heavenly Father forgiven you?

10. Love does not delight in evil

How many times have I told my children "I told you so!"?

We can even seem happy that our children have received a natural consequence for their actions. Proverbs 24:17 says "Do not gloat when your enemy falls; when they stumble, do not let your heart rejoice." If we are to treat our enemy with this kind of respect, how can we rejoice when our children, who we love, fail?

Confession time… after all, this is Erica from Confessions of a Homeschooler.

Shamefully my husband and I have willingly agreed to let our children do something simply because we knew our kids would disobey between now and then and we could take it away as a consequence!

I think in legal terms that's called "entrapment". And then when the inevitable happens, we are thankful and rejoice that we didn't have to endure yet another birthday party at Chucked-Up-Cheese!

However, delighting in our children's failures is not supporting them, encouraging them, or lifting them up!

So instead now we do our best to set them up for success by guiding them, reminding them, and teaching them to be responsible.

We can't expect that they always know the best choices to make even though it may seem obvious to us as adults. Remember they're kids; they are self-serving, self-seeking bundles of joy that need constant discipleship to stay on task!

Now, I'm most definitely NOT telling you to set your children up for failure. However I am saying that there are plenty of teachable moments when raising your children if you just pay attention to them.

Seize the day parent.

Seize the day.

11. Love rejoices in truth

"How often do I point out my child's faults?"

"How often do I point out their success?"

On an average day, how many positive and negative comments do we make in regards to our children? Most of us can easily answer that the majority of our comments are negative. "Do this; don't do that", or "What were you thinking?"

Remember to pray for wisdom regarding your children. Ask God to give you His love for your kids. Ask Him to show you what their strengths are so you can encourage your child in those areas. You can even ask Him to show you how you can use things like strong willed behavior for good!

Let your children know that God has given them all gifts, seek out what those gifts are and praise and encourage them in that!

"The fear of the Lord is the beginning of knowledge." ~Proverbs 9:10

12. Love always protects

Am I faithful to support my children and have their backs in all things?

Galatians 6:2 says "Carry each other's burdens, and in this way you will fulfill the law of Christ."

Let's be sure to help our children in whatever area they are lacking. Help them to be responsible, remind them to do the things that are required of them, show them how to be faithful. It is our job to train and disciple our children. They don't come out of the box knowing how to act and what to do. It's a bummer. I know our job would be so much easier if they did!

13. Love always trusts

Do I trust my children or hold past deceptions against them?

Have a willingness to always pursue a trusting relationship with our children. Lying can drive a spike into any relationship, and knowing that our children have deceived us can be very hurtful. That's why it's important to be consistent in discipline. Create a plan for discipline in your family. If you have an agreed upon plan for discipline in your household you will be more successful in avoiding lying and deception between you and your children.

In our house we have a double consequence for lying. Remember when dealing with this that we have all lied, we've probably even lied to our children at some point. Be firm on this rule, but remember that love does not keep hold of bitterness!

Romans 5:5 states "Now hope does not disappoint, because the love of God has been poured out in our hearts by the Holy Spirit who was given to us."

(You can download a discipline chart on my website www.confessionsofahomeschooler.com then click on 'Organization' then on 'Tips for Moms'.)

14. Love endures all things

Do our children know that we love them?

Do they have a false expectation that our love is conditional depending on their behavior?

I remember talking to my 4 year old one night because she said that I didn't love her anymore. I said, "Don't you know that Mom and Dad love you no matter what you do?" She sadly replied, "No".

That broke my heart!

From that point on, whenever she disobeys I am careful to let her know that I still love her no matter what bad choices she's making. I also made sure that she knew that Jesus loves her no matter what, as well. Our love for our children should be un-conditional. Our children can easily take our anger towards them as a sign of our lack of love for them.

Take some time today and make sure that your kids know that you love them through all circumstances, and that you will never leave nor forsake them, just as our heavenly Father will never leave nor forsake us!

15. Love always perseveres

Go all in.
Not half way.
All in.

Colossians 3:21 says "Fathers [mothers], do not provoke your children, lest they become discouraged."

As ministers of our family it is our God given calling to train up our children in the way they should go *(Proverbs 22:6)*. We can impart the same grace we have been given to our children, showing them that we are in this for the long haul.

We can stick with them through their trials and give them the security knowing that they aren't going through life on their own. If something isn't working in our home we have the power and authority to change it. If something's causing us or our children frustration, find a way to guide them through it.

I spent the first couple years of our homeschooling with the attitude that we were "trying it out". I knew that if I failed we could just stick the kids in school and be done with it. I wasn't fully committed to our decision to homeschool or to my kids' education. Once I decided to go all in, our school came alive. I think God was up there breathing a sigh of relief that I've finally accepted His calling!

Whatever you do, do it as unto the Lord.

"Whatever you do, work at it with all your heart, as working for the Lord, not for human masters." -Colossians 3:23

16. Love never fails

God gives us everything we need to disciple and train our children.

God gave us our children knowing how foolish we are, but He also gave us the answers that will give us the ability to succeed in this journey. He wants us to pray for our needs, letting us know that whatever we pray for in His name he will give us. We may, and probably will, fail. But He never fails us. His love and guidance will carry us through on this journey.

As a parent, don't let your love ever fail. No matter what trials you face with your children or your spouse. Stand firm in love for them. Support and encourage them. Be there when they need help. Be their #1 cheerleader.

Taking Action

Spend some extra time in prayer this week. Ask God to help you in any area you are lacking when it comes to following 1 Corinthians 13 in your home.

Pray for help over areas that need change, and the perseverance and strength to change them as well!

Here are some extra ideas to help build your relationship with your child:

- Have a regular "date night" with each of your children to encourage communication.
- Encourage them often!
- Foster an honest and open relationship. (i.e. talk regularly!)
- Tell them you love them daily.
- Be consistent with discipline.
- Be slow to anger
- Show them patience just as God has had patience with you.
- Encourage and help them to persevere through trials.
- Teach and model forgiveness.
- Practice kindness in your home.
- Honor others above yourself.

8

Preparing Your Heart

"I have hidden Your Word in my heart that I might not sin against you." - Psalm 119:11

Preparing your own heart is crucial when raising children. If I am to face a day of sibling squabbles and character development all with a spirit of patience, then I need help!

Despite what others may think, I was not born naturally patient. When people hear we homeschool, their first comment is usually something along the lines of this:

"Wow, you must be really patient!"

I usually respond with something like this, "Not at all, but that would be nice!"

As a matter of fact I'm probably one of the least patient people I know. But as long as I start my day out with guidance from God, He gets me through the daily trials that are to come.

I often look at other families and wonder how those parents who seem to have it all together manage it?

Are you laughing right now because you thought I had it all together?

Well I don't.

So now you know, I'm not patient, and I don't have it all together. And keeping things running smoothly is something that I struggle with.

S-T-R-U-G-G-L-E.

However, I figure it must be worth it or it wouldn't be such a struggle, so I persevere. My advice to you is to start your day in the Word. Some days get started off right and flow so well that I vow to start my day off in the Word for the rest of my life.

Then tomorrow comes…and something happens…like the baby decides to take her diaper off and smear poop all over…which causes me to leap out of bed and land into a day of disasters. So yes, it is a daily struggle.

How then does this homeschooling mom of 4 manage to stay sane? Well, let's start with my dream scenario. I like dreaming. Plus, things always work out in my dreams.

Aaah…I start the day off being awaken gently by the whispering of my husband who has informed me that he's gotten up with all the children and they are downstairs finishing dishes from breakfast and beginning their morning devotions. He tells me to take a few minutes to myself and spend some time in the Word before I begin my morning routine.

There's a sweet little red-breasted bird outside my window singing a welcoming song to the sun as I crack open my velvety soft Bible, and begin to soak in the richness of Jesus. I spend quality time in the Word with no distractions, then another half hour in prayer.

After that I meander to the shower where I get refreshed and ready for the day ahead. I saunter down to the kitchen where I find all 4 of my children. They are sitting at the table discussing ways they can be kind to one another today after reading through Ephesians 4:32.

We spend the afternoon as a family sitting beneath a large oak tree, listening to a gentle stream flowing by as we read through the gospel of Matthew. We spend time together, laughing and just having fun before heading home for a wholesome home-cooked meal (apparently cooked by fairies since I've been by the stream all day).

The kids graciously offer to get themselves ready for bed, and then my husband and I spend a few minutes with each child individually asking how their day went, and just listening to them as they talk soaking in every minute of our time together. Alas, the day is done and my husband and I have some free time to relax and enjoy each other's company before the next dawn arises."

I really should just end my day there, but in the spirit of keeping it real I'd just like to say that dream has never happened in real life. Well, at least not the quite peaceful image that story portrays.

I've resigned myself to the fact that the term "quiet time" just may not apply to my life right now. As a matter of fact when you have four children inhabiting your home the term "quiet" isn't exactly…um…accurate.

Despite my efforts, I tend to stay up way too late at night in order to get out of bed with my little red breasted friend tweeting out my window each morning.

So planning early morning devotion time never seems to work out so well for me. *I know, I know, you have to work at it…and I am…it's on my "to-do" list.*

Honestly some days the only devotions I actually get are the ones that I do with my kids.

And do you know what?

I think that's okay. It's a season that I'm in and I am absolutely blessed through the time we spend together in the Word. Now, I do still aim for my own time alone with God, it's just that some days it's hard to come by, and so for me it ends up usually being done at night.

I wouldn't entirely suggest the night-time plan as I often find myself thinking "Well, I really could've used that encouragement about 8 hours ago!" But sometimes you have to take what you can get right now.

I realize that my children are not going to be with me for very long and so spending time with them, especially in God's Word is precious! Once I came to this realization it really changed my view of "quiet time"!

Instead of hiding in the laundry room in order to get just 2 minutes of peace, I've decided to include my children in my quiet time. After all, if I'm to be a model for my children, and if they never see me doing quiet time or leading them in habit, how are they supposed to know what to do?

Taking Action

Here are a few ways we are able to have some quiet time each day. I've found the easier I make it on myself, the more likely I am to follow through!

Daily Bible Time

Every afternoon we all grab our own Bible for reading time. Everyone finds a spot on the couch and we read silently to ourselves. It's like a corporate quiet time if you will. Our preschooler has her own bible and she mostly just looks at pictures and such, but she's still required to be quiet during this time.

This doesn't need to be overly complicated; as a matter of fact I encourage you to keep it simple.

Sometimes we do a family devotional together. And sometimes we take a time to focus on some character training. Other times it can be as simple as reading from the Word together.

"So shall My word be that goes forth from My mouth; It shall not return to Me void, but it shall accomplish what I please, and it shall prosper in the thing for which I sent it." Isaiah 55:11

Verse of the Day

Pick a verse for the day, and keep your bible open to it. Leave the bible on your kitchen counter, or somewhere that you frequent. Each time you walk by, read your verse again and think of a way to apply it to what's going on today. Feel free to read the passage out loud to your children too. It's a great reminder to them as well.

Sticky Notes

Write encouraging verses on post-it-notes and stick them on the refrigerator, bathroom mirrors, and in your car. Make it a game with your children to see who can find the hidden verses for the day.

Seize the Time!

I have found that there is at least one point of time in each day where I find myself with literally a few free minutes. The kids are playing happily and I'm contemplating my next move. When this time comes,

I challenge you to pull out your Bible and take that opportunity to spend a few precious minutes with your Jesus. Make sure you have some lying around in rooms you frequent, so you don't have any excuses. I consider this my first fruits, the first time of the day where I'm not overwhelmed with demands. I have a choice to either give that time to God, or to something else.

Pray for God's help

I pray constantly. I know it may sound ironic but I also pray that God will remind me to get into the Word. Some days get so hectic that I literally forget until I crawl into bed at night and start to relax. Suddenly I realize that I've not even so much as cracked my Bible!

Now I keep a small Bible by my bedside so that I can grab it easily for days such as this. While we're on the topic, make sure to keep in prayer all through the day. Constant communication with God will make your relationship stronger!

Keep a Bible in your car

As a matter of fact keep a Bible anywhere you tend to frequent.

I know it sounds funny, but I do my best to help myself out whenever possible. In an attempt to set myself up for success, we have Bibles all over the house and one in our cars. I also have one on my iPhone, so that I have the opportunity to get into the Word, even if it's just for a few minutes.

Keeping our family in God's Word has not only brought us closer together, but it also helps prepare our hearts on a daily basis. As we seek to reach the hearts of our children, we're building a lasting relationship with them. And that relationship will allow us to become the primary influence in their heart and their lives.

9

Priorities, Priorities!

"In their hearts humans plan their course, but the Lord establishes their steps." ~ Proverbs 16:9

As a parent our time is stretched thin. Whether we are working, or staying at home, time is one thing most of us do not have a lot of during any given day.

If our child's education is truly a priority to us, then we will give them our most precious commodity, our TIME.

Assessing our Commitments

I want to take a short moment to talk about our time as parents. In Proverbs 19:21 it says "Many are the plans in a person's heart, but it is the Lord's purpose that prevails."

For the most part, we can control where we spend the majority of our time. Aside from work, we have hobbies, interests, commitments, and the like that slowly eat away at our days, weeks, and years. And where we choose to spend our time, is where we spend our soul.

Our children are typically only in our homes for approximately 18 years. After that they leave our nest and venture off into their own lives. For most of us that leaves a good 30+ years of no kids in our homes. When I think about it this way, suddenly my time with my children becomes much more precious to me.

> "Many are the plans in a person's heart, but it is the Lord's purpose that prevails."
>
> Proverbs 19:21

Let's think back to when we discussed parenting as a ministry. Take a minute to pray for an open heart. Next, I want you to sit down and make a list of all of your commitments and hobbies that you currently have.

Consider things like school, serving at church, leading a bible study, volunteering at girl/boy scouts, scrapbooking, golfing, and so on. List any commitments you have made that take your time away from your family. Also list any commitments that you have set for your whole family such as sports, extracurricular activities, school events, etc.

Next, note if the commitment is outside or inside the home, and then a brief explanation stating if this commitment benefits, or takes away from your family. Finally, give the commitment a priority. 1 for less priority, 5 for highest priority.

(You can download a printable copy of the commitment worksheet from www.ConfessionsofaHomeschooler.com. Click on 'Organization' and 'Tips for Moms'.)

Commitments	Time Spent
Work	40 hours
Church	2 hours
Email	5 hours
Hobbies	3 hours
House Chores	4 hours
Other	5 hours

When your list is complete, sit down with your spouse (if possible), and go over your commitments. See if there are any items on there that can be removed. Pray over the list together, and let God lead you. He will make it clear where you are to be spending your time.

One thing I constantly struggle with is balance. I am a "yes" person, and I tend to volunteer for everything! But I'm going to share some wisdom imparted to me from a mentor of mine. She once told me "Erica, there are a million worthy causes, but you can't do them all." It has stuck with me all these years, and God is kind enough to bring it back to my attention when I start getting crazy with my commitments!

"You can do anything, but not everything."
-David Allen

I mentioned before that I'm a people pleaser. I'm also a "yes" person. I have a very hard time telling people no. You need a new website? Sure! You need a new logo and business cards? No problem. You need me to make a meal for a sick friend? Of course!

All of those are worthy causes, but the truth is that I have responsibilities that need to remain my primary focus. Educating our children at home is obviously my top priority. Family, blogging, and sharing encouragement with others is another. Whatever other opportunities arise, no matter how noble they seem, need to be taken into careful consideration.

I'm currently reading through The Best Yes by Lysa Terkeurst. If you're an over committed people pleaser like me and haven't read it, I highly suggest picking it up once you're done with this book. It's all about learning how to honor God with the time we have.

God has laid out plans for each of us. We need to be in constant prayer, making sure that we've been really seeking His direction in our commitments.

We need to be open to the fact that even though it may be something we WANT to do. God may not have that thing for us at this time. By us saying "no" to something we are not called to, He can open up the door for someone else to say "yes".

Please don't misunderstand, I still do things with friends, serve at our church, and have hobbies. But after learning my lesson the hard way, and I did learn it the HARD way...God made it very clear to me that my first ministry was at home. I am now much more careful about what I say "yes" to. If it's something that will take us away from our home, then my husband and I discuss it, and decide if it is worth it to our family before we commit.

The same thing goes for your children's commitments. If they are spending 90% of their time outside of your home, it will be difficult for you to be their primary influence. Instead they will be led by their teachers, coaches, and peers. That is not to say that they should not participate in extracurricular activities. I'd just like to suggest that you limit them to activities they are truly passionate about and reserve time to gather as a family frequently.

With four children, this can be a difficult task. For the time being we've allowed each of our children to do one sport per season. Thankfully some of these overlap. For example all three of our daughters are participating in a dance class. The lessons are all on the same day at the same location.

All four of them participate in swimming in which lessons occur twice a week at the same time and in the same location. My son participates in summer sports while the girls dance is on break. All of these choices have helped to keep us together as a family. They have also prevented us from spending half our lives in the car.

Taking Action

What are some of the things that suck up our time? I challenge you to sit down and make a simple list of your main commitments, hobbies, and anything else that can distract you from your time with your family.

First, list the things you do on a daily basis and a general amount of time that you spend on them. The commitment chart on the following page is just a sample of what your activities might look like.

Next make a list of extra-curricular or hobby type activities you do and how much time you spend there as well. This maybe more of a weekly or monthly list than a daily one.

Once you're all done listing things you're involved in (the things in my chart are simply examples), take a look at where you're time is going.

Is it common for you to get caught up on Facebook or other social media?

Do you get lost in long phone conversations or games on those fancy new smart phones that are so prevalent in our world?

Do you prefer to take your weekends for golf or scrapbooking instead of spending time with your family?

All of these are warning signs that your family may be suffering from lack of quality time together.

Now, please don't email me with hate mail. I am not talking about an occasional golf outing, or shopping trip. But when these behaviors become a priority over spending time with your children I encourage you to take a look at your priorities and make any necessary changes that will instead benefit your family as a whole.

Remember as I mentioned before, your children will only be with you a short time. Make the most of it now.

Also take a minute to note of your child's commitments. Just like us, your children can be easily over-committed as well. Are you allowing them to spend too much time away from the home?

For example if they're in school all day, then sports all evening, how much time on a daily basis do they actually spend with your family? As parents I think it's important to encourage a connected family-centered environment.

If you're feeling stressed out about their schedule, chances are they're feeling stressed about it as well.

While this may not be a popular choice at first, limiting children's sports and activities will soon be a blessing to your family. Not only will you be spending less time chauffeuring everyone around, but you'll actually be learning more about one another, engaging with each other, and otherwise building a solid family relationship with your children.

While I'm all about encouraging my children in their interests, I try not to let things like sports and extra-curricular activities dictate the goings-on of our family. As with any commitment, we find it best to discuss the matters as a family. Then as parents, we will ultimately decide what is best for our family at that time.

A great test to access your inter-family relationship is to take your family out to dinner. Take a look around the table. If everyone is playing individually on an electronic device, take that as a sign that your family needs a change.

If you as the parent are investing your time into your child, they'll begin to do the same as well. Pretty soon you'll be enjoying family dinners without electronics and instead you'll be having actual conversations with one another.

Encouraging Family Time

When we first had children, my husband and I sat down and asked ourselves "What do we want our children to look like when they've finished their formal education?"

In Luke 2:52 it says "And Jesus grew in wisdom and in stature, and in favor with God and men."

We agreed that our desire is for our children to learn to trust in the Word of God, to have it hidden in their heart. (Psalm 119:11) We want to train them in the way they should go, so it may go well with them. (Proverbs 22:6)

We want them to be healthy, confident, and to know they are fearfully and wonderfully made. (Psalm 139:14) We want them to keep their childlike faith. (Matthew 18:3) And we want them to be a light in this world. (Matthew 5:6)

We want them to "always be prepared to give an answer to everyone who asks [them] to give the reason for the hope that [they] have. But do this with gentleness and respect." (1 Peter 3:15)

We want them to be confident, to have good manners, to be compassionate, to be respectful, and to be humble in spirit.

That's a tall order for a teacher, coach, or Sunday school teacher, and frankly it's a tall order for a parent as well. Honestly, I'm not even close to qualified to meet those goals. But God is, and I am grateful that He will equip us and work through us, rather than have to depend on myself.

So how do we go about imparting all of this wisdom to our children? The answer is easy.

We spend time with them.
We teach them.

We love them.
We encourage them.
We share God's Word with them.

Time is one of the most precious commodities of all. None of us are guaranteed tomorrow, and so we must live for today.

James 4:14 says "Why, you do not even know what will happen tomorrow. What is your life? You are a mist that appears for a little while and then vanishes."

Children naturally seek out our time. I often find myself shooing my children away because I'm "right in the middle of something." But if we're always right in the middle of something, then all our children will ever hear is "maybe later". They will learn to assume that other things are more important to you than they are.

While we may not like to think about it, like I mentioned before, none of us are guaranteed tomorrow. That includes our children. We have some dear friends who lost their son at a very early age to an unexpected and unexplainable health issue. Had they not spent their life pouring into him, they would have regretted that the rest of their days.

Lord willing, our children do live to have a full life, what will we leave behind with them? Obviously, we all face the same fate. Instead of leaving behind unequipped children who have not been properly sent out into the world, we have the beautiful opportunity to leave behind a Godly legacy within our children that will be passed down for generations to come.

10

Teaching Responsibility to Children

"His master replied, 'Well done, good and faithful servant! You have been faithful with a few things; I will put you in charge of many things. Come and share your master's happiness!" - Matthew 25:21

How many of you feel like you've been hit by a bus the end of the day? It's okay you can raise your hands this is all anonymous.

How many of you can barely find the time to read this book? Even though I assure you that this book will be so riveting that you can't bear put it down.

Well, we're going to take the edge off of your chronic fatigue syndrome which will in turn benefit your parenting by teaching your children responsibility. At the same time it helps relieve the stress you've been feeling trying to manage everything on your own. Now instead of thinking about those toilets that need to be cleaned you'll be alert and focused during your day!

God's Word tells us that "Moreover it is required in stewards that one be found faithful." -1 Corinthians 4:2

It is important to teach our children to be thankful for all that God has blessed our family with. 1 Thessalonian 5:18 says "Give thanks in all circumstances, for this is God's will for you in Christ Jesus."

Teaching Responsibility...

We all want to hear those blessed words "Well done, good and faithful servant". Let's take that and bring it into the home!

Whether you have a little, or a lot, God has blessed you! It helps we look at our possessions as God's, not as our own. So then, how are we to take care of the things He has blessed us with?

If God gave us a gift would we toss it on the floor? Step on it? Allow it to get broken, dirty, and finally thrown away? Heavens no! We would be extra careful to take good care that we treated it with the utmost respect.

Our homes, our furniture, our toys, our animals, and our siblings are all gifts from God. They are not ours, they belong to Him, and we have received them out of love from our Lord. Let's take care of them!

Note: If you haven't done my character study on being a good steward, now might be a good time to check it out! You can download a copy on my website at www.confessionsofahomeschooler.com.

(Click 'Organization', 'Posts by Subject', and then 'Character Studies'.)

Giving Responsibilities

Part of teaching children responsibility lies with actually giving them responsibilities! I know it sounds silly, but so many of us doubt our child's ability to do things that we inadvertently do chores for them that they're certainly capable of.

Oh, my beloved chore-chart, how I love thee! Ever since implementing and being consistent with chores, my life has been...well, simply beautiful. Not only do my kids LOVE this thing, but I literally LOVE this thing right back!

(You can download your own free chore chart from my website at www.confessionsofahomeschooler.com, click on 'Organization', then 'Tips for Moms'.)

The idea behind this is simple. God has given us a house full of things to take care of so let's be faithful! Each of our children are given approximately 4 chores per day to complete. When they complete their chore, they turn the card backwards. At the end of the day I give them 1 ticket for each chore completed, which they can later redeem for a prize. The older children are required to do their chores each day and instead of getting reimbursed with a prize they are given a set allowance at the end of each week.

To keep things simple I have an app on my phone that automatically adds their weekly allowance. If they have a week where they do not complete their cards I can easily deduct from their balance. I can also add or deduct from their account if they purchase something or get money from another source.

My kids love the chore chart setup. They like knowing what is expected of them for the day, and they really like knowing that they'll be rewarded for their hard work at the end of the day. I like that things get done. Instead of having kids who were once destroying our sanctuary, they are now helping to take care of it!

Please don't get me wrong, I am not a child laborer by any means. We promote teamwork in our home, but if for whatever reason they choose not to do a chore, they simply don't get a ticket. My system is conveniently arranged so that they are rewarded for work they do, and not for work they don't do. If they don't choose to do their chores, they don't get a prize. It's as simple as that.

And, if mom or dad has to do their chore, then we get their ticket. This can later be redeemed for a morsel from the top secret chocolate prize box...shhh!

Discipline in the Home

It is my belief that the real meat of parenting is the character training of our children. The academics are important and will come, but one of the huge benefits to spending time with our children is that we are present for all of the discipline "opportunities" during our child's time with us.

As parents we have the choice to stop what we are doing and address their behavior right away. Or we can ignore it and allow it to continue. When we teach our children about honesty, respect, and compassion, we in turn reach their hearts and change them from the inside out.

Anyone can command obedience, but seeking to change your child's heart will carry on into their adult life, the lives of their children, and grandchildren after them.

I don't know about you, but I find that the times when I lose my temper with my children are completely my fault. It happens because instead of stopping what I'm doing and dealing with the situation at hand, I let it escalate until I finally can't take it anymore. By the time I stop what I'm doing to discipline them I'm angry and ready to yell.

All of that can be avoided by simply stopping and addressing the problem right away.

Let's take what we've learned about being a minister to our family and apply that to how we view the discipline of our children. It totally changes our perspective when we realize that we are simply carrying out God's will for His children whom he has entrusted to us. The discipline of our children is God's way of encouraging, motivating, and steering them in the right direction. Just as He so patiently does with us.

> "Anyone can command obedience, but seeking to change your child's heart will carry on into their adult life, the lives of their children, and grandchildren after them." - Erica

Changing our perspective takes some of the pressure off of us to be what the world deems good parents. It allows us to parent and teach with intention as servants of God. Out of love for our children we faithfully follow God's plan for their lives.

One way to accomplish this task is through consistent discipline and structure in our homes.

House Rules

In order to raise our children with intention, we need a game plan. So we have created a set of rules that we agreed to follow as a family to make our home run smoothly. Again if we have not set goals, then not only do our kids not know what our expectations are, but neither do we.

In an attempt to retain some semblance of order and sanity in our household, my husband and I came up with a set of family rules that we follow.

House Rules...

Once we set the rules and consequences, my husband called a family meeting. We presented the new rules to our children along with the decided upon consequence, asked if anyone had any questions and let them know the new rules were in effect immediately.

I have to say this has been the best thing we've done for our family yet. First, it took all the pressure off of me to be the bad guy; after all I'm just following through with the rules.

Second, it keeps me from going overboard emotionally because the kids are acting up and I can't think of a consequence for their behavior on the fly.

Third, it seemed to give all of us some sense of comfort and stability knowing what our expectations for our family are.

I encourage you to sit down with your spouse *(if possible)* and create a list of family rules. You can also use the goals you set for your home to help define what is important to your family. I encourage you to keep the rules fairly simple. Our family has 7 main rules. You can see a sample of our family rules on my website, and I also have a free printable form to give you a starting point.

(You can download an editable version of the family rules on my website at www.confessionsofahomeschooler.com then click on 'Free Printables', then 'Mom Stuff'.)

Taking Action

Coming up with family rules might sound overwhelming, but stick to what's important and keep it simple. The easier they are to remember the better your family will follow the rules. First, sit down with your spouse (if possible) and discuss rules that you'd both like to see applied.

Here's how we organize them:

1. What is the rule? For example, a rule might be to respect Mom and Dad. You will then want to give a couple of examples of what that means. For example how you talk in a kind tone of voice, etc.
2. What is the discipline or consequence for breaking the rule? You and your spouse should agree on an appropriate consequence. It is typically helpful if

the consequence is somehow related to the rule. For example if your rule is no TV after 5pm, your consequence for breaking this rule might be to take TV away from the rule breaker for the rest of the week depending on their age.

3. What is the supporting Scripture? As I've stressed in the days leading up to today, we need a reason, plan, and guidance for what we are doing. It is much easier to explain to your child why a rule is important, if you yourself know why. The supporting scripture just reminds us what God's Word says on the topic so we can be faithful and just to carry out His commands.

Since implementing our household and discipline rules, we've found that time-out's just don't really cut it for the older kids. We wanted something a little more effective when dealing with disobedience and poor behavior. Since my chore chart has been received so well, I decided to add in some discipline cards. These should be things that you really don't enjoy doing, but that still need to get done.

We use these cards as a consequence for disobedience and sometimes poor behavior choices with our children. If they make a bad choice, they pull a discipline card from a jar. They are expected to complete that discipline, then follow through with whatever they were asked to do originally. If they refuse to complete their discipline card, they get what's called a motivator, something such as losing TV privileges, or their Nintendo DS or whatever is of value to them at that time.

If one of the children receives a discipline card during the day, it goes behind their name on our Chore Chart once they are finished. This way when Dad comes home, he can see who has had a bad day and he can discuss it with them if necessary.

I included one card called "Help Mom Cook". This is our mercy card. Most kids like to help cook, and we want to show them what mercy means by allowing them to receive something that they do not deserve.

I really hope you all take the time to do this, consistency in discipline is key to getting and keeping your home in order.

(You can download an editable version of the family rules on my website at www.confessionsofahomeschooler.com then click on 'Organization', then 'Tips for Moms'.)

11

How do I do it all?

"Therefore, my beloved brothers, be steadfast, immovable, always abounding in the work of the Lord, knowing that in the Lord your labor is not in vain." ~ 1 Corinthians 15:58

Now you might be wondering why there is a chapter about "doing it all" in a book about children's education. However, I firmly believe that creating a well-functioning home will model valuable organizational skills to your children. This, in turn, will aid them in their adult lives when they eventually take charge of their own homes.

This is a topic I've received several emails on, as well. People always want to know how I "do it all".

You know...homeschool, cook, clean, do laundry, write curriculum, blog, chauffer kids all around town, and generally stay sane.

After I got done laughing hysterically, I thought I should just be honest and lay it out for you.

So this is me keeping it real.

The short answer is that I don't.

The long answer is organization.

I know it may seem like things are all perfect over here at the Confessions home, but you have to keep one thing in mind when reading my blog, and really this goes for most blogs in general.

You only see what I *want* you to see.

You don't see the messes my youngest makes while we're trying to do school. And trust me, she makes messes. It's her specialty.

I often take my arm, or foot and sweep it across the floor clearing away all the debris so I can snap a lovely shot of one of my children working happily on a project.

You don't see my laundry room. Ever. Enough said.

With 6 people in our house, it seems like that humming sound coming from the laundry room never stops. There used to be folded clothes on top of the washer and dryer, piles of dirty clothes ready to be washed, and a full dryer that I was previously avoiding, until instituting my beloved chore chart. Now we do one load a day, and we share in the folding responsibility. Everyone puts their own clothes away, even my 5 year old.

You don't see the failed crafts, burnt cooking experiments, and all of my "brilliant ideas gone awry".

No I don't blog those things. Instead I prefer to block it out and pretend it never happened.

I think people have unrealistic expectations about what it's like in a bloggers home. They see all the pretty, but I want to take this time to assure you that it's probably just as crazy at our home as it is at yours!

So, how do I do it all?

First off, no one can do it all. No one has ever done it all. And no one ever will do it all.

So the first thing you can do is give yourself a break. Something has to give, and for me it's usually the cleaning, my sanity, dinner...or all 3 depending on the day.

Remember, the only pressure we're under is pressure we've put on ourselves. If your schedule's too hectic, take a minute, and write down all your commitments. I know, I know, you don't have a minute, but trust me this will help. Actually you should've already done this if you've read this far.

Next see what you can get rid of, and what you want to keep. Often times we've simply over committed to things that sounded great at the time, but don't work so well in the reality of our daily lives.

If we're constantly rushing around like a chicken with our heads cut off, be assured your children will grow up to follow suit. But if we can establish a good and realistic schedule for our family, it will benefit everyone.

The children will be less stressed out, and we will as well. That also allows us some breathing room to enjoy our family for those precious years that we have our children under our roof.

You can rest assured that my house is just as chaotic as yours, but one thing we have started to help out is our daily schedule. We have a basic daily routine that we follow. It is constantly in flux, but adding a general structure to your day can help things go much more smoothly.

The best way I find to combat feeling like a failure, like I'm not doing enough, like I'm dropping balls, is to focus on who I am in Christ. Let's take a look at who God says we are.

- You are saved by grace through faith. (Ephesians 2:8-9)
- You are an ambassador for Christ. (Corinthians 5:20)
- You are an heir of God. (Romans 8:17)
- You are created in His image. (Genesis 1:27)
- You are beloved. (Colossians 3:12)
- You are created for good works. (Ephesians 2:10)
- You are chosen. (1 peter 2:9)

Those are but a few verses of who we are in God's eyes, but I think that is a good start, don't you? Best of all, I don't see any to-do lists other than to be grateful for all that God has done for me.

Create a Family Schedule

Start off by creating your own family schedule. Make this a basic overview of family commitments for each day of the week. You might choose to color code each family member so you can easily see who is doing what.

By writing down basics it is much easier to see where you have time, and where you may be overbooked. Keep this calendar in a handy place so you can refer to it frequently when more opportunities arise.

> "Many are the plans in a person's heart, but it is the Lord's purpose that prevails."
>
> -Proverbs 19:21

Although you don't have to stick to this plan like glue, it is nice to have a basic daily schedule posted so everyone can quickly see what is going on. I've also noticed my children checking this frequently to see what's coming up next.

This is not something that has to be written in stone, but having a schedule will help guide you through your day, week, and ultimately, your year.

Kids tend to thrive on consistency and structure as well, so having a daily schedule will help keep everyone focused and on task. It can be a simple routine such as breakfast, school, chores, free time, dinner, and bed time. Or it can be more detailed to include extracurricular activities and events. As you determine your schedule, make sure it is realistic for your family.

Take heed of how many opportunities you agree to. It can be easy to over-do it. So just be careful to keep a healthy balance when assessing your commitments.

Share your schedule with your children, and then hang it somewhere visible in the home. You can be as rigid or flexible as you need to be here, but at least you'll have a general plan to shoot for. Keeping the schedule is up to you.

The other part includes learning to be flexible. If an amazing opportunity arises, take a look at your schedule and determine if you have the leeway to take it. Being flexible allows us to venture away from our "plan" and actually enjoy life with our family.

"Many are the plans in a person's heart, but it is the Lord's purpose that prevails." ~ Proverbs 19:21

Taking Action

Good time management for any family is a necessity for getting your home in order. In the next chapter we'll discuss a bit more on schedules and structure in your home. But there are a few more tips

I'd like to share with you on the topic of time management, and keeping your sanity.

First of all, no one can "do it all" so to speak. As I mentioned already, something usually has to give when you're juggling school, running a household, parenting children, being a spouse, serving in ministry, working, and the list goes on.

Remember, the only pressure we're under is pressure we've taken on ourselves. So make any necessary changes to your schedule and move forward.

Having some sort of routine that you follow will go a long way to helping you stay above water. Good time management is crucial to both your mental and physical well-being.

Now, your schedule won't necessarily look like mine. You probably have much different commitments, needs, and family interests. But I do encourage you to take some time today to focus on making a schedule that works for your family, and fits your unique needs.

Make sure to write it down on paper, or create one that can be printed. That way you can hang it somewhere in your home where it can be seen easily and referred to as needed.

This will do wonders for keeping everyone on task!

12

Schedules & Structure

"But all things should be done decently and in order." ~ 1 Corinthians 14:40

When I started this chapter, I did an internet search on bible verses pertaining to order and organization. Being a type A personality, you can imagine my glee when I happened upon this gem! I hadn't ever seen this verse before, but I'm so glad that I did! Now, in context this verse is referring to the worship of God, and that it should be done in order.

But moving on in my search I discovered a common theme repeated often. God is not the God of confusion, but of peace. (1 Corinthians 14:33) It is God who establishes our steps, directs our paths, and leads our family.

Since God is one of order, I can only infer that my home should reflect that to a certain extent as well.

As I previously mentioned, my kids thrive on schedule and structure, and if you can't tell by now, I do as well. This type of personality is a blessing, but also has its pitfalls as well. The main thing I want to share with you is to be open to the leading of the Holy Spirit in your day.

We can trust God to lead us in everything and that includes our daily schedules as well.

Will I get my laundry done?
Will my house get cleaned?
When will my child have time to get homework completed?
How are we going to get through today?
Ack! It's 5pm, what are we having for dinner?

Have you found yourself asking any of these questions? I've found that having a schedule, even if I don't stick to it, provides me and my children with a much needed sense of structure. Having our days planned out for us helps to alleviate some of the chaos surrounding our home.

I've asked myself all of these questions more than once, and have found out that only through planning ahead can they be answered. Is it critical to get the laundry done? Maybe, maybe not, but at least if you have a plan you know that the never ending loads will actually get done at some point.

Another thing that always stresses me out is meal time. I actually like to cook, but I'm just not that exactly gifted in this area, so having some sort of plan that guides me is a huge blessing.

I've been sharing my Monthly Meal Plans on my blog over the last few years. I don't always follow them exactly, but they are a great guide. And that's okay, because I have a plan. If I deviate it's on purpose. Although my kids seem to like the meal plan too and often complain when I don't follow it!

I also shop off my monthly meal plan. I go to the grocery store each week and get only what's on our schedule for meals for that week. This has helped reduce my grocery bill, as well as ensure I have needed items to make the meals.

No more standing in front of the refrigerator at 5pm wishing I had a little genie to pop out and make us dinner!

That's great you say, but what about everything else? What about the vacuuming, laundry, toilets, mopping…you know, all the daily chores that need to get done? Most of those get done during chore time, the kids and I all do something from our Chore Chart after school is done each day. We do keep our home picked up during the week, but the deep cleaning usually happens on the weekend. We put on some music, give each person one area they're in charge of, and we get at it.

You can be as rigid or flexible as you need to be here, but at least you'll have a general plan to shoot for. Chores and meals and everything else will get done later.

If you're a working parent, or your children attend school outside of the home having a schedule will be even more critical. There are not as many hours available to you to get everything done. Having things like meals planned ahead of time, scheduled homework hours, and chore times will help take some of the chaos out of your daily life.

Our Daily Schedule

Just for a little light humor I thought I'd share, in a nutshell, what we do each day...please don't judge.

- 7:30-8:00 am: Wake up, pray, take shower, keep praying, get dressed, pray some more: I seriously do not leave my room until all these things are done. If I did, I don't think I'd ever get back to my room to shower and that would be bad. *And once I started smelling bad enough, I'd have no friends to talk me off of the proverbial parenting ledge.*
- 8:15 am: Throw in a load of laundry.
- 8:16 am: Wonder how it's possible that so much laundry has accumulated overnight.
- 8:30 am: Make breakfast, read kids their devotion while we're eating.
- 9:00 am: Start school, track down the students, re-start school, track down 1st grader, re-start school, track down preschooler, lock all kids in schoolroom, finish school.

- Noon: Swap out laundry, lunch, kids get free time while I clean lunch dishes. Start dishwasher so whoever has that chore can empty it before dinner.
- 12:45 pm: Start afternoon school subjects.
- 2:00-ish: School's Out! Check Email, catch up on work stuff.
- 3:00 pm: Chore time, finish any chores left for day
- 5:30 pm: Dinner followed by clean up and Dad time with kids
- 7:30 pm: Start bedtime routine
- 8:00 pm: Breathe a sigh of relief that I made it through another day of parenting and homeschooling…aaaah….check calendar to see how many more school days are left…pray for perseverance.
- 8:30 pm: Work a little, chat with husband, and chill out.
- 9:00 pm: Rinse and repeat.

Do I always follow this plan?

Yes and no.

I do try to stick to our daily plan, mostly as a means of staying sane. But the kids also seem to do better when we stick to a fairly routine schedule. However, I am flexible to change things that aren't working, and make changes where needed. Each day has its own variations. But on most given days I follow what I set out to do.

Like I always say, "Better to have a plan and not need it, than to need a plan and not have it!"

Actually that quote originated from my husband whose motto is: "Better to have it and not need it, than need it and not have it."

This applies anytime we leave the house.

It's why I have a mini-van with a large capacity rear storage area.

Taking Action

Take some time today to jot down a basic family schedule. Color code by person if you need to, but that way you can create a working calendar of events so that you can keep everyone up to date on activities, and make sure you aren't over committing.

13

Plate Spinning 101

"Unless the Lord builds the house, its builder's labor in vain." ~Psalm 127:1

Here is where the rubber meets the road my friend.

Once you've made all of the important decisions the direction your family will follow, it's time to commit to them.

I'm queen of starting something, and not finishing. I always have good intentions. But life can easily get in the way.

Decide what will be priorities for your family and focus on those first. Once you have taken care of the big things, you can have the freedom to welcome other smaller things into your day knowing that you've met your major goals. If you decide to let something minor go that day, it will be okay as you've taken care of the things you previously set forth as a priority.

Remember, saying no is okay. If you've scheduled family time, don't be tempted to skip out on it because something else pops up. Keep that as a priority on your list.

Whether you are a stay at home parent, or a working parent, it is common to feel like you've got a thousand plates spinning all at once and can't seem to keep up. For any parent this can be an overwhelming thought, with the big question being "How do I keep everything running smoothly?"

> The Big Question is...
>
> "How do I keep all my plates in the air, and in what order do I spin them?"

In other words, "How do I keep all of my plates in the air, and in what order do I spin them?"

I just want to be clear that this book isn't some fool-proof master plan. It's just how I keep those little men in little white coats from coming to take me away. However I do want to give you an action list that can help alleviate some of the stress in your everyday life.

Taking Action

First, list your plates.

Take a few minutes and list all of the things you have going on right now that require your attention. Here are mine...God, husband, children, homeschool, family time, animals (2 dogs, 1 cat, 4 fish, 2 sweet birds), blogging/writing, cooking, cleaning, laundry, extracurricular activities, time with friends, and me time. *(Oh yeah right...)*

Second, prioritize!

Take a few minutes to prioritize your commitments listed previously. Take care of the big priorities first, and then let the rest fit in where they can. You can see how I have set up the priorities for our family below to give you a starting point.

Third... simplify.

Take a look at all of your plates, pray for wisdom to know what God has for you right now, and what He doesn't. Don't waste your time on things that God isn't in, you'll just be spinning your plates in vain! Pair down your commitments to just those things that are most important to your family. Remember to plan in some free time so you can have a little breathing room, and enjoy time together.

Psalm 127:1 "Unless the Lord builds the house, its builder's labor in vain."

Our Priorities

Here is a list of our priorities. Of course this is just a guide, something to help you get started. Your plates will vary according to your unique needs.

God

"But seek first His kingdom and His righteousness, and all these things will be given to you as well." ~Matthew 6:33

At times like this, it's important to keep things in perspective. If everything else gets pushed aside today, will it really matter? So what if the laundry sits for the day? So what if I order in food instead of making dinner here and there? So what if we take a day off school? Really, in order to keep all the plates of life spinning, we have to make priorities. The first one must be time with God. Setting a priority on God's will for our lives will naturally pass down to your children as they see you spending regular time with Him.

In regards to homeschool, if we don't get anything else done, I at least try to make it a priority that we do our Bible time. Now, I'm preaching to myself here, because for me this is the easiest to let slide, and I can easily forget about it until I go to bed, then instantly I realize that I forgot to do my devotion. I've made a deal with myself that if this happens, I will get up, turn on the light and do it, right then and there. Better late than never I say. I also use this motto to justify starting school late.

Marriage

This is important parents; husbands/wives must come before kids. And I think it's important for kids to see that your husband/wife has priority. Your spouse will be there long after the kids are gone, and while there is a definite season when kids seem to prevail in order due to sheer necessity, it's still important to recognize that your spouse should be your priority.

Marriage was the first institution created by God… "For this reason a man will leave his father and mother and be united to his wife, and they will become one flesh." -Genesis 2:24

Therefore, if God placed that importance on marriage, than so shall we! When my husband comes home, he tries to greet me first, then the kids. After that the kids are sent to the other room to play for a few minutes so we can have some time to discuss whatever is needed without yelling over all the loudness that comes with having four children.

Well, except for our 5 year old, nothing can keep her from her daddy when he first walks in. Did I mention my other motto: "Blessed are the flexible"?

Children

These little guys are nothing more than treasures in heaven! It is our job to, "Train a child in the way he should go, and when he is old he will not turn from it." -Proverbs 22:6

God has given us the greatest gift ever, and it blows my mind that He's entrusted *us* to raise one of his precious children, not to mention four of them! Sometimes I just scratch my head and wonder what God was doing when He made this choice, but then I'm reminded that He knows what He's doing regardless of whether or not I do! And praise God for that! I try to make an effort to spend a little bit of time each day 1-on-1 with each child. It can be as easy as sitting my 4 year old on the counter to keep me company while I make dinner, to reading with my 7 year old at night. Whatever it is, take a couple minutes each day to personally tell your children that you love spending time with them!

Education

We truly believe we are called to homeschool our children, you can read more about it on my website. But I will say this; giving priority to our children's education has GREATLY impacted the quality and flow of our days. As I previously mentioned, I was in denial regarding our calling to homeschool. I was constantly telling myself if it didn't go well, we'd just put our children in school. Finally I came to accept our choice and really made our children's education a priority.

Simply committing to our decision and making it a priority has made all of the difference for our family. Whatever your choice of education is, be committed!

Animals

We have 2 dogs, 1 cat, 4 fish, and 2 birds. I know...crazy right? This one was easy though...I delegate! I have 4 kids; surely they can manage to help feed the animals! Presto, one less plate for mom! Go Me!

Taking care of our animals is one of the items included in our chore chart. And the fewer chores we as parents have to do, the more time we have to play with the kiddos. This is a good motivator, because after all, most kids want your time.

Blogging

When I first started my blog back in 2009, I only intended it as a means to keep family updated on our daily lives. But as my blog grew, I realized that it had become a ministry to other parents and homeschooling families.

It became a place of encouragement, ideas, tips, resources, and help for homeschooling families as well as school teachers.

It was not through my amazing vision, or brilliant business plan that this came about. Instead it was God who used a plain homeschooling mama to help reach thousands all across the world with His message for them.

Now it is an important part of our family life. My kids, husband, and my mom all participate and help in running my blog. It is His ministry, we are grateful to be a part of it, and it is definitely on my priority list.

Cooking

As I mentioned I'm not exactly gifted in the culinary arts. But we have to eat right?

Thus was birthed the monthly meal plans. I'm thankful for these, and yes, I do use them.

If you're like me, you might want to consider monthly meal planning or freezer meals to help you get through long and busy days.

I have a friend who spends one day a month cooking freezer meals, and then doesn't cook the rest of the month! I haven't been able to accomplish this just yet, but if you have a friend it'd be a fun mom's day and a great way to get some serious prepared dinners done!

(You can download monthly meal plans on my website under 'Recipes'.)

Family Time

In today's society, family time has to be a priority! Since my husband is away from home working all day, we do our best to make sure we eat dinner each night as a family. We also have a bedtime routine which we try to follow.

I stress “try” because it doesn’t always go down like this, but like I say “Better to have a plan and not follow it, than to not have a plan at all!” Sound familiar?

Our goal is for both my husband and I to do bedtime together. We give baths, brush teeth, cuddle with the kids, etc. Then we all gather as a family on our bed and read a family devotion, pray, then off to bed for the munchkins.

I think it’s all too easy to forgo family time and let everyone do their own activities without realizing the long term effects this can have on your relationships.

Dinner time is also a great way to gather the whole family.

Cleaning

I happen to be a neat freak, and I can’t handle clutter. This proves to be a challenge with having four kiddos, and homeschooling. We literally live in our home. 24 hours a day. Someone is here, making some sort of mess. However, my clean-freak tendencies also help to keep our house somewhat orderly. We do a fun thing called “Ten Minute Tidy”; this is where we run around like mad putting away anything found on the floor before Daddy gets home. We set a timer and it’s like a race!

> We like to put on some music while we’re cleaning to make it more fun!

We also make it a habit to pick up the house regularly so it doesn't become too overwhelming.

Now before you start thinking I'm some kind of super-mom, let me assure you that I am not! And I'd bet my bottom dollar that, at the end of the day there's at least 1 toy on the floor in each room, even if it's hidden under the couch.

For our main household cleaning, we work as a team. The older children help with vacuuming, dusting, and general housework, cleaning their rooms, dishes, etc. Working together to take care of the home God has given you teaches responsibility, team work, and good stewardship. These tasks are divided up based on what is appropriate for your child's age.

We like to put on some music while we're cleaning to make it more fun.

Laundry and other household chores

Oh the dreaded laundry! Even after explaining to my kids that they don't need to change 5 times a day, they still seem to rack up the piles. Now that they're a *little* older, even the five year old helps in putting her clothes away. Laundry is an important life skill, so I taught them early on how to run the washer and dryer.

However I usually supervise this as pouring liquid soap into the washing machine cup seems to be so much fun that one doesn't want to stop pouring even though the "fill to here" line has clearly been reached.

I'm sure people handle this differently, however I chose to do one load a day. It's not as overwhelming as doing 20 loads on Saturday and it's less scary for the kids (and me) to put away a couple outfits as opposed to a whole week's worth!

Psst...The laundry is a great thing to add to your family chore chart.

Kid's Activities

We decided to allow each of our children one activity at a time. Since we homeschool, we are more flexible for things that meet during the daytime. While we allow our children to do extracurricular activities we are also careful to make sure we have family time together with our daddy. We also don't want to be consistently rushing from one thing to the next, thereby causing "stress" for our children and me.

Finally....time with friends and ME time!

Sorry, but I've searched diligently, and unfortunately "me time" is nowhere to be found in the Bible! Well, technically it is there, it's just listed as selfishness.

The good news is that if you start off with plate #1, time with God, He will give you the rest you need! And He'll even throw in some "me time" when He knows I need it most. And here's the proof so you don't have to take my word for it.

"Come to Me all you who are weary and burdened, and I will give you rest." ~ Matthew 11:28

I am also fortunate to have a husband who understands the need for a periodic 'girls night out' as well. I have a wonderful group of supportive friends who gather regularly for coffee and chit-chat. We encourage one another, and support each other through our journey as women, and as mothers.

Now, looking back you can see that I have about 12 virtual plates spinning at all times.

Frankly, that's a tad overwhelming.

> "Come to me all you who are weary and burdened, and I will give you rest."
>
> *-Matthew 11:28*

Remember being flexible is key. You are in charge of your family. It is OKAY to skip an activity here and there. You are not required by some invisible law to participate in everything that your friends and neighbors do. It's okay to say no.

Observe how crazy the lives of overcommitted families are and learn from them!

Take note of your plates and make any necessary adjustments. Then keep them in mind as other things arise.

The point here is to be flexible, open to what God has for your family for this season. Then you can rest in the confidence of knowing that you have set God's priorities in place for your life, so that when a plate falls…and they will…it's not one of the big ones.

14

Making an Educational Decision

"The fear of the Lord is the beginning of wisdom, and knowledge of the Holy One is understanding." ~Proverbs 9:10

"If any of you lacks wisdom, you should ask God, who gives generously to all without finding fault, and it will be given to you." ~James 1:5

None of us are perfect parents, and we all have made mistakes. But hopefully by now, you've gotten the point that your child's future starts at home.

And it starts with you.

Your child's education is not just about academics, but about discipling them. It's something that will impact their entire lives and should not be taken lightly.

That said, these days there are a lot of options for us now regarding our child's education.

So far we've discussed building a solid relationship with your child. We've covered the character building part of their development. We've talked about setting them up for success beginning in the home.

So now I'd like to move on by discussing some of the things to consider when choosing their academic path.

Like I mentioned before, we have obviously chosen to homeschool our children. But I know that option is not for everyone. So how do you decide what path to follow for your own family?

Here are a few tangible ways to help you get started on making an informed and purposeful decision regarding your children's education.

Before you get overwhelmed with all of the choices out there, I encourage you to stop and take a minute to breathe. Below are some steps you can take to help make the decision process a lot less painful. They will also help you be more confident in your final choice, and parent intentionally instead of aimlessly.

Pray

First I suggest that you come together with your spouse (if possible) and pray over this decision. I encourage you to be in prayer over this long before school becomes a reality. Trying to make a last minute decision isn't wise in this area.

Both traditional schooling and homeschooling require time to prepare on your part, and your child's. Seek God's will for your family, your children's future, and their educational needs, and He will direct your paths.

Assess the Situation

Second, create a list of all of your financial responsibilities, social commitments, your family priorities, and your child's specific needs. Then seek to find a schooling mode that fits all of those needs, or at least as closely as possible.

For example if you have a special needs student, homeschooling might be a good option for you. Or if both you and your spouse work outside the home, traditional school might be your best option.

If you are a single parent, you may have commitments that will somewhat guide your choice as well. If you're wondering, yes, you can successfully homeschool as a single parent. I have a whole chapter in my Homeschooling 101 book that is dedicated to homeschooling as a single parent where you can read more on the topic.

Make a Plan

Once you've prayed for direction and researched all of your available options, it's time to make a plan. We will discuss this in more detail in the following chapter. But at the most basic level, start charting out the goals and educational vision that you have for your family.

Research institutions that fit those goals, then apply to your choice of school or send in a letter of intent to homeschool. And start moving forward with your plan knowing you've done your research and made the best decision you can.

Be Flexible

Even the most well laid plans, can go wrong.

Even the best of intentions might not work out.

Our children are all unique in their own way. Their academic needs will differ as well. I know many families who started out with kids in the public school system only to remove them to homeschool. I have friends who homeschooled and later put their children into school as their needs changed.

Whatever choices you make, be prepared that they might not work out as you expected. Commit to your plan, but remember to be flexible enough to realize when a change is needed. That way you will be open to doing whatever is best for your family and your children.

But whatever you do, don't compare yourself to your friend, neighbor, or family. Each family's needs are unique.

Taking Charge of your Child's Education

"Train up a child in the way he should go; even when he is old he will not depart from it." -Proverbs 22:6

By now you know that education is more than just passing on academic knowledge. Instead, I encourage you to think of education as imparting your ethical, moral, and character values to your child.

Sure, they need to learn academics skills, and depending on their life goals, they'll also need to get into a school of higher education. But education isn't just about textbooks.

While they certainly will get various academic skills from a school or home education environment, we don't want to let the 'village' actually raise our children. That responsibility falls directly on us. If our students are not doing well in the educational choice we've committed them to, it is our calling to figure out how to best help them through it.

That may mean changing schools, bringing them home, or making some other change that will create a more successful educational experience for them.

As parents, we have been given a unique blessing from God. We are responsible for training up our children. We can share our beliefs, values, and ethics with our children. We can teach them how to cope with various trials life throws at us.

"Don't let the Village raise your child."

We also help develop good character in our children by teaching them the proper way to relate to those around them. We show them how to treat others, serving them, and honoring them. We teach them now to share, and be selfless. And we show them how to properly handle conflict as it arises.

But all of those things must come from within the home first. We cannot solely depend upon teachers, administrators, coaches, and Sunday school teachers to be the primary influence in our children's lives. God called us to have that role and responsibility in the lives of the children He has blessed us with.

"Only be careful, and watch yourselves closely so that you do not forget the things your eyes have seen or let them slip from your heart as long as you live.

Teach them to your children and to their children after them." -Deuteronomy 4:9

That said it can be difficult to go against the grain of society. There are a lot of passionate debates about which school is the finest, which educational choice is the best, and whose students are the most well-rounded and successful.

It's evident in all of the "My child is an honor student at…fill in the blank here", bumper stickers we see on the roads these days. While it's typically just a proud parent praising their children, seeing those can be a catalyst to others to make sure their student is also the best. Suddenly we feel pressure to make sure that our children are also keeping up with, or better yet excelling over, other students.

We put our children in the best schools with the best teachers, the best classes, and the best extra-curricular options. We make sure they are on the path to graduate with honors. All in an attempt to make sure they have a solid education and become successful adults.

But at what cost does all of this pressure come? What if our child is being led down a path other than what we've come to expect? Are we still open to encouraging them?

My hope is yes. That we will encourage them, cheer for them, pick them up when they fall, and teach them the perseverance it takes to truly become successful no matter their life goals. For some this might mean making a less than popular educational choice. But if we shy away from worrying about what others will think, and instead take charge of our child's education based on their individual needs, then we can be sure that we're truly doing what is best for our own families.

I know when we told people we were homeschooling we got several concerned looks. Some even said a few less than kind words regarding our decision. For many it took several years to be able to see that we weren't "ruining" our children. But that they were intelligent, friendly, and outgoing children, who were thriving within our educational choice.

Remember that what is best for your friend's family isn't necessarily what is best for yours. Forget keeping up with the Joneses. Set a vision for your family and make choices based on that.

Taking Action

Today we have more choices than ever regarding educational environments for our children. Here are a few things to consider when you begin thinking about your child's future and begin making educational choices.

Education isn't always best handled by "The Experts". You are your child's number one influence. As parents we often feel like the experts know more than we do about our child, or can do a better job at teaching them.

No one loves your child more than you, nor will they show your child the one-on-one attention and patience that you will. With 20-30 students in most public school classrooms even the most dedicated teachers cannot provide the individual care and compassion that they would like to.

So keep in mind that whatever decision you make, you as the parent will still need to be a key asset to the development of your child's education.

1. Know Your Educational Options. There are currently five options when it comes to the education of a child. Public Schools, Charter Schools, Private Schools, Online/Virtual schools, and Homeschooling. Research the options available to help you make the best decision for both your child and your family. We'll cover these options in more depth later on in this chapter.

2. Know Your Child's Needs. Are there areas your child is excelling in and areas they need more assistance in? By catering your child's educational needs you can help give them a leg up in their academic future.

3. Consider finances. Whether we like it or not, finances can be a large factor when choosing which educational option is best for our children and our family. Some private schools may be simply out of our budget. Alternatively, we might be able to make some budgetary changes that will allow us to direct more of our income towards our children's education.

Public School

Many people choose public school because it's free and it's convenient. Most communities have a public school within reasonable driving distance and many offer bus services to get your kiddos to school. Some things to consider when choosing a public school are its academic ratings, as well as average class size.

Most schools will have their ratings available online. Along with academic statistics, they will also share information on bullying, drug violations, weapon citations, and more. All of these things should greatly influence your choice of school.

While many public schools have excellent programs, class size is something to consider. If the school is overly full, students will get much less one-on-one instruction, and can easily fall behind, or become bored with learning.

Charter School

Charter schools are basically public schools that receive public funding, but are not governed by many of the state laws that regulate public schools. They tend to focus more on specific academic subject areas such as mathematics and reading that exceeds some of the expectations of state funded public schools.

Most have limited enrollment and tend to attract students who are already stronger. With a more challenging class load students who struggle may fall even further behind in this setting.

Private School

Private schools tend to be expensive, but they also provide a great balance between traditional academics and core religious values. They also have the ability to control their enrollment making it easier for them to keep a more ideal class size.

Private schools are not governed by state laws or standards like public schools are. This allows them to create their own standards. You'll want to determine if the school's agenda is in alignment with your own when picking a private school option.

Virtual/Online Education

One of the newest educational options is the online or virtual school. Essentially this type of education is public school via the internet. Students attend school in the comfort of their own home. It might be beneficial for students struggling in a traditional school setting.

It can also be beneficial for the parent. Since online schooling is done via internet, there is still a teacher for your child. Students simply do the work at home, then turn in assignments via email or an online software. They are then graded and returned to you via the internet.

Many of these virtual schools provide all of the required curriculum and even a computer which can help out financially.

Homeschooling

Homeschooling, or home-based schooling, is definitely on the rise as an educational option for many families. Homeschooling affords many benefits for both families and children individually. Via homeschooling, parents can tailor their curriculum so it best fits the needs of their children. They also have the flexibility to do more extra activities such as field trips, hands-on activities, and real life experiences that can be limited by the confines of a more traditional school setting.

Despite what many parents think, having a teaching degree is not required to homeschool your children. The vast curriculum choices available make teaching your child at home easier than ever.

While you don't have to be a lawyer to homeschool, you will at the very least need a basic knowledge of your state laws and requirements for homeschooling. Each state is different, so you'll want to make sure that you are following your specific state requirements.

The best place to learn about your state's homeschooling laws is by visiting the Homeschool Legal Defense Association (www.hslda.org). They have current homeschooling information, laws, and general information on getting started, as well.

I also have a book, Homeschooling 101: A guide to getting started, which covers everything you need to know to get started on your homeschooling journey.

Don't Compare Yourself

No matter how perfect another family may appear, I'm here to tell you that no family is perfect, except the one that is obeying God's will.

When making an educational decision for your children, do not allow yourself to be influenced or discouraged by falling into the trap of comparison. The reality of it is that everyone learns at different levels. And each of us has different needs when it comes to receiving the best education possible.

Your children may be above the national standard, or right on grade level academically speaking and that is okay. They may also have delays or special needs, again it is okay.

They may be ahead in math, but delayed in reading. Yep, it's still okay.

Let me say that again.

It's okay.

Each one of our children is different and the beauty of parenting is that we have the ability to take charge of our child's education and meet their unique needs. Thereby giving the best possible learning environment we can.

So ignore the 'Joneses'. Instead, keep your focus on the needs of your own unique family.

Like I've already mentioned, don't let the proverbial 'village' determine what is best for your child. Instead pray about what God is calling you to, and make choices that directly relate to the goals and vision you've set for your own family.

16

Taking Charge in Your Homeschool

"But as for me and my household, we will serve the Lord."
-Joshua 24:15

As homeschoolers, we have a unique opportunity to be with our children all the time. We can quickly address character issues and other problems almost immediately.

But be careful. Even though we are with our children all day long, that doesn't mean we are spending quality time with them.

Once when my children were asking me to play a game with them, I responded, "We just got done doing school all day together!"

To that they replied, "Yeah, but that doesn't count as spending time with us!"

Wow.

I'd never thought of it that way. They don't just want our time, but they want to spend quality time with us. That doesn't mean it has to cost a lot of money, or be super complicated. For my children right now, they're totally content with some snuggle time. They love to sit and read a book together. Most of my kids just like to do things with me. That can be anything from going to the grocery store together, stopping in at a local coffee shop, or taking a walk together and discussing our day.

Whatever it is, make sure you spend some time just talking with your kids, listening to them. Ask them about their day, and really just show an overall interest in their life.

As homeschoolers we can also take charge in tangible ways. For example by not letting our curriculum run our homeschool. We currently have the freedom to pick our own curriculum, and choose things that will most benefit our child's needs.

We can tailor their education to fit our children specifically. So don't let your curriculum dictate your homeschool, but instead make sure you dictate the curriculum. As you choose your curriculum for the year, pray over the best fit for your family and your child's needs.

Then just remember to be flexible enough to make changes as needed so that you are remaining in control over your homeschooling experience.

Taking Action

- Create a schedule that works for your family's needs.
- Take charge over the curriculum you plan to use. Keeping in mind state requirements.
- Adjust the curriculum to fit your needs. You do not have to follow a curriculum exactly, and that includes its predetermined schedule.
- Choose curriculum that is fun and interesting to your children.
- Help foster an environment of learning by allowing children to experiment, experience, and do things on their own.
- Spend quality "fun" time with your children each day!
- Plan field trips and outings that help reach your homeschooling goals, while at the same time engage your children in hands-on ways!

17

Getting Involved in Your Child's Education

"But as for you, continue in what you have learned and have firmly believed, knowing from whom you learned it and how from childhood you have been acquainted with the sacred writings, which are able to make you wise for salvation through faith in Christ Jesus." -2 Timothy 3:14-15 (ESV)

No matter what your educational choices for your family are, it's important to stay involved in every aspect of your child's education.

Staying engaged with our children is usually one of our highest priorities, but with the hustle and bustle of life it can often become secondary. It's typically something you didn't even notice, but before you know it you've lost touch with what is going on in your child's life. Especially as students get older, parents tend to lean on teachers more and more to manage their child's education. Instead of allowing your child's progress to slip between the cracks I challenge you to stay in touch.

There are numerous benefits to getting involved in your child's education, some of which include higher grades, better behavior, improved education, increased confidence, and stronger family bonds.

According to a study conducted by the National Education Association, regardless of family income or background, students with involved parents were more likely to have higher grades, be promoted, pass classes, attend school regularly, have better social skills, better behavior, and to graduate then go on to a postsecondary education.

Taking an active role in your child's education, and really their life, is one of the best ways to boost your youngster's chances of success. Studies show that parental involvement has tremendous impact on not only your child's academic achievements, but also social and life skills as well.

Every little bit counts, so even if you're feeling like you don't have a ton of time to volunteer at your child's school, your child will still benefit from even a few hours a year. And you can also take an active support roll with their homework by simply being available in the evenings for discussion and guidance.

The result of any time you spend with your child is that you're there for them, encouraging them, and invested in their lives. It's never too late to get started!

Taking Action

Here are some great ways to take charge of your child's education no matter where they attend school.

Communicate Frequently

Speak to your child, their teachers, and administrators to find out where you can help serve and get involved in your child's school. Keep in close contact with teachers so you have a good relationship with them.

Most educators are happy to help students whose parents show an involvement in their education. One of the number one complaints from teachers is that parents leave it all up to them and are not willing to take part in their child's lives. Work together with your student's teacher to come up with educational materials and programs that might help benefit your student's progress.

If you are homeschooling, talk to your spouse and children often so they know how they are doing, what areas need improvement, and what, if anything, needs to be changed to improve your homeschooling.

Ask questions regularly

Ask if there is something you can do at home to help your student if they are struggling in a certain area. There is no reason why you should have to wait for a report card to find out how your child is doing in school. Your teacher should be more than willing to let you know how your student is progressing in their class and any areas that can use improvement.

As a homeschooling family, access your child's grades regularly. Find out if they're struggling in a specific area and make any necessary changes to help your child be successful.

Some questions to keep in mind:

- What specifically will your child be learning this year?
- What will most affect their grades (tests, classroom work, projects, etc.)?
- Is there additional help available if needed?
- What is the best way to stay informed of your child's progress?
- What can I do outside of school work to help them succeed?

Help your child set goals

Work with your child and their teachers to set specific and attainable goals. If they're struggling in a certain area, make that a priority. If they have a specific interest in another area, encourage them there as well.

Setting goals for your child is a great way to help give them a sense of accomplishment, as well as inspire them to do their best. It can also encourage them to overcome obstacles in areas of weakness.

Setting goals can also be as simple as helping them come up with a realistic schedule. Making a checklist of things they need to get done on any given day, or keeping a day planner to help them stay organized.

Build a Relationship

Keep in close relationship with your child as well. Talk to them about their struggles, both academically and personally. Make it a point to insert yourself into your child's life so they know you care about them. The more time you invest in your child, the more likely they are to come to you when they encounter trials in their life.

Be Available

Be available for your child, not only for extra-curricular functions, but also make time for your child on a daily basis to discuss their lives. This gives you, as the parent, an opportunity to help your child solve their issues in a way that is in line with your own morals and values.

Like I mentioned before, just because you may be a homeschooler, don't assume you're spending quality time with your children! Ask them, and make sure to create time for them. If your children attend a more traditional school make it a priority to communicate with them daily. Talk about their day, their classes, and any successes or struggles they may be having.

Monitor Schoolwork

Part of growing up is learning to be responsible for one self. While older students might be expected to be liable for keeping track of their own work, younger students can benefit greatly from a little help. Often they will bring home tons of paperwork and they may have even stuffed it all into their backpacks haphazardly. Help them go through their work and file or sort as needed.

Help show them how to manage their workload, and give them the proper tools to organize the paper work themselves as well. Encourage them to clean out their work, and keep anything that is due in a specific location so it doesn't get misplaced.

A great idea is a different folder for every subject. That way when they come to that subject, they can pull out that particular folder or binder, keep everything together, and then put it back when that subject is completed.

If you homeschool, show your children how to organize their work area, and keep everything clean and put away in the proper place. That way they aren't searching for lost papers, missing assignments, and the like.

They might even benefit from instruction on how to create a task list that they can check off each day to make sure they are completing the necessary assignments. A great way to do this is to give your child a planner. That way they can keep anything important written down in an easily accessible location. They can check off things as they are completed and will reduce the tendency to "forget" something.

The added bonus of monitoring their work, is that you will also know how they're doing and can take any action needed to help get them back on track before it's too late. And it's always a great idea to have good communication with their teachers as well, so everyone is on the same page.

Make good use of technology

We are living in a technological world and you can use this to your advantage to stay connected to your child's school. Most schools offer email, websites, and newsletters for students as well as parents. Now more than ever we have access to more information and we are capable of having better connection with our teachers than ever before.

Volunteer

Teachers are typically looking for willing parents to help chaperone field trips, help with school events, and even help with administrative work for their classes. While this takes time, making yourself available to help serve in your child's school, will increase your connection to your child's education. If you have the time, volunteer to help in their classroom as well.

If your child is in a public school, joining the PTA is a great way to stay up to date on school information and activities for your child. If you don't have time to volunteer during the week, see if there is anything you can do from home or on weekends.

Make Conferences a Priority

Most schools have frequent conferences, and parent-teacher meetings to keep you informed of your child's progress. Make these a priority and ask questions. This is a great opportunity to help steer your child in the right direction before it's too late.

If you homeschool, or are involved in a co-op, talk to the teachers there as well. Make sure to hold regular meetings at home with your child to discuss their progress, and any areas that might need improvement.

You don't want to hit your child with a bad report card at the end of the year when it's too late for them to make any changes.

Get Connected

Whether you've chosen to put your child in a school system or homeschool, getting connected to other parents is an excellent way to stay in touch, share advice, and stay involved in your child's learning experience.

Make an effort to meet other parents and establish a chain of support!

Get Involved

As I mentioned already, studies show that when parents are involved in their child's educational experience the child will tend to have better attendance *(if they're in traditional school)*, increased self-esteem, decreased drug use, higher grades, better tests scores, better graduation rates, and greater enrollment rates in a post-secondary education. *(See information on the National Parent Teacher Association in the Bibliography section.)*

But aside from all of the academic benefits, I encourage you to get involved in your child's life because it will build your relationship, it will strengthen your family, and it will help encourage your child to be the best person they can be.

12 Ways to a Good Start

"If any of you lacks wisdom, you should ask God, who gives generously to all without finding fault, and it will be given to you." - James 1:5

We tend to forget that having a successful day can depend on much more than the classes we're in, or the teachers we have. But so many factors at home can greatly influence the dynamics of not only our day, but also our response to trials that we may face as well.

As we've discussed already teaching character traits, values, and morals to your child can greatly help them face each day as it comes. I often tell my children, "You can't control what happens, but you can control your reaction to it."

Along with all of these normal stresses in life, I have found a few tangible tips that can help give your child a head start to a successful day, year, and life!

Let's start the day off on the right foot shall we? It's not only important to the kiddos, but mom and dad included!

Here are a few ways we try to get a good start in our home…

Taking Action

Good Nutrition

Start with a healthy breakfast. Taking a few minutes each morning to start your child's day with a healthy breakfast is a great way to encourage them to have a successful day. Pack a healthy lunch for your child so they are receiving a well-balanced diet.

A great way to save time, and morning rush chaos, is to prepare lunches the night before. You might also consider making several freezer meals that you can pull out for a healthy dinner even when you don't have time to cook.

On my blog I have several recipe plans, and monthly freezer meal suggestions to help you get started. You can see them under the "Recipes" tab on my website.

Promote Self-Confidence

Leave your child with a hug, kiss, and encouraging send off. Telling your child you love them and are proud of them is an excellent way to boost self-esteem.

Make sure to take the time to talk with them after their day as well. We like to do this before bed time when everyone is calmed down for the day. We discuss how the day went, what they had struggles with, and what things went well for them.

Keeping in constant communication with your child will not only improve your relationship with them, but will also foster trust between you. When your child has a real problem they will be much more likely to confide in you for help.

Teach Responsibility

Teach them responsibility; however also stay up to date on homework, assignments, etc. so they are well prepared for their day and not scrambling at the last minute to complete a project. This goes double for homeschoolers. Many times since we homeschool, I find myself getting relaxed about assignments being due. True to form, kids will get away with whatever you let them! So now we are fairly strict on getting work turned in on time. Just as if they were in a traditional school, they will have a consequence if work is turned in messy or late.

Create an organized area for school supplies

There's nothing like fumbling around in the morning looking for backpacks, shoes, homework assignments, etc. Keeping your child's area clutter-free and organized will eliminate a lot of stress in the morning time.

I suggest having a special location for each child's belongings. They are responsible for keeping their shoes, coats, and backpacks in their proper location. That way in the morning things will be easily located and ready to go.

Make their space functional

Create an organized work area for your child to do homework or school work if they're homeschooling. Just as we have a hard time focusing on work when we are surrounded by chaos, children are also easily distracted by these things. Making sure they have a decent work area to focus and complete their work is essential to having a successful day. You might even consider having a special area setup for them to work. Whatever you do, try to have some sort of place with adequate lighting, workspace, and supplies to set up your student for success with homework or school work.

I would also encourage you to remove as many distractions as possible while they're working. That might be no electronics, cell phones, TV, etc.

Make school/homework part of your daily routine

As a homeschooler we don't have homework very often, but we do need to be diligent in doing our school work. Create a working schedule and stick to it. While we have the ability to be more flexible in our routine, too much flexibility can lead to missed school days. Be diligent to your school work and make sure to get it completed each day.

If your child is in a traditional school system, chances are they will have homework most days. Don't wait for them to tell you what they have, make homework time a priority and set a daily time for it. If there are sporting events, do it afterwards, but always make sure to discuss their assignments with them so they are getting their work completed.

If you find your child is frustrated or having a poor attitude during homework time, you might consider giving them a break after they get home from school before beginning work. We usually have a snack, and then allow free play if time allows before we move on to any evening sports or homework time just to give their brains a bit of a recharge.

Talk and Listen

Make time for your child at the end of each day. Instead of checking email, talking on the phone, or reading your mail, make time to talk one-on-one with your child. Ask how their day went, what they did, if they had any issues, or good news to report.

Keeping the lines of communication open between you and your child will make a difference when they face challenges. It can't be something that is only followed through on during trials, but instead must be a long standing relationship built between the two of you.

I mentioned adding a snack in the previous section, and this snack time is a great opportunity to casually chat about their day!

Limit Electronics

In today's world this can be difficult to do, however I encourage you to limit the amount of time you allow your child to partake in TV, video games, iPhones, Facebook, and the like. Instead encourage family time, game nights, family bike rides, and other activities that protect your relationships instead of promoting the separation of family that can come from the online world.

Extra-Curricular Activities

Extra-curricular activities are a great way to get your child involved in team sports, get specific training for their interests, and help them get some physical exercise too! Unfortunately so often I see parents dropping their children off at sporting events then leaving. Whenever possible I make it a priority to stay and watch practices, attend games, recitals, and special events our children are involved in. Not only will it make your child feel good to see you making time for their interests, but it will also show them they are important to you and take a priority in your life.

Set a bed time and stick to it

Having a regular schedule includes both getting up on time, and going to bed on time. Often we're more laid back about our children's bedtime, however getting enough sleep is critical to their daily performance and well-being.

If your child is involved in extra-curricular activities, make sure they're not over committed. Getting home late only to have hours of homework to complete is a recipe for an exhausted child. Set a reasonable bedtime, and help your children stick to it, even when they don't want to!

Setting goals

Setting goals is an excellent way of teaching your child to overcome any hurdles they may face by taking them one step at a time.

Help your child establish age appropriate targets, and then come up with a plan for working towards them. Let your child be involved in this process, and have a say in what they would like to accomplish as well. A goal can be something as simple as completing a homework assignment, to something more long term such as learning to play a musical instrument.

Start by discussing a fun goal they can achieve within a short amount of time. Help them create a realistic schedule to get to their goal. Next help hold them accountable as they progress through the schedule. And finally applaud their effort. Even if they didn't make their goal, encourage them, and tell them how impressed you are by their effort. If they didn't quite attain their goals, review it with them. Maybe the schedule was too vague, or unrealistic. Discuss suggestions for improvements, and try again, or glean that knowledge for future endeavors.

As students learn to set goals for themselves, things that might have previously been overwhelming. Things like moving from a C to an A in math, winning a science fair, or playing an instrument, might now be more attainable.

Have an eternal outlook

Being an involved parent takes time and energy on your part. It isn't an easy job by any means and often means you will have to put some of your needs and desires to the side. It means re-thinking your priorities and often involves sacrificing your own desires for those of your child.

But I encourage you to think of this time with eternity in mind. Raising a child is a short season in our lives and while it can be overwhelming at the time, it will be over before we know it.

On average your child will only spend 18 years in your home. That's only a fraction of your lifetime.

Don't let your child leave your home with regrets on how your time was spent.

Instead launch them into the world knowing you have raised them in the way they should go so when they are old they will not fall.

"Train up a child in the way he should go, and when he is old he will not depart from it." ~ Proverbs 22:6

19

Helping Your Special Needs Child

"By wisdom a house is built, and by understanding it is established; by knowledge the rooms are filled with all rare and beautiful treasures." -Proverbs 24:3-4

First off, I want to encourage you that you are not alone! Not only are there a variety of special needs types out there, but there are just as many online helps as well.

That said your child's needs are probably still unique. The needs may range from something such as attention deficit disorder to children with more severe and multiple handicaps.

Often bringing special needs children home to be educated is a wonderful way to reach an otherwise reluctant student. But there are also plenty of wonderful traditional school options that offer special needs programs that can greatly benefit your child as well.

As their parent you have the ability to offer your student the security, stability, flexibility, and encouragement they need to be successful.

Whether you choose to homeschool, or take advantage of more traditional schooling there are many ways you can help your special needs child be successful in their academic lives.

Taking Action

Get a good start

In addition to the suggestions in the previous chapter, helping your special needs child prepare for their day is a necessity!

Make sure to help your child prepare the night before school. Get their bag ready, make sure assignments are neatly placed in their notebook, and completed. Hang everything in a special spot in your home, so in the morning your child can gather their belongings easily.

If necessary, lay outfits out the night before as well, just so that is one less thing they need to worry about when getting ready for their day. This sense of order will help your child feel more in control of their day.

And of course, prepare a nutritious breakfast so they're ready for the day ahead!

Go through their backpack regularly

Make sure to help remind them of assignments due, keep papers organized, and supplies filled and appropriate for their daily needs.

You might even create an organizational method that works best for them. Things like color coded folders, special pouches for supplies, and reminder lists can all help guide them through their day.

If you're homeschooling, don't assume these things will be taken care of. Make a visual reminder list of all of your student's tasks for the day so they can learn to be responsible for their assignments as well.

Help them memorize their schedule

By creating a visual schedule you can easily help your child know what's expected of them each day. It also serves as a reminder of what they've done already, and what's to come. This sense of structure can be very comforting to your special needs student.

An easy way to do this is to create simple 3x5 cards with pictures and possibly a check box on them. Next punch a hole in the top corner of the cards, and put them on a key ring. These can be easily attached to your child's backpack so they don't get lost. If you laminate them you re-use them each day and they are more durable!

Be their biggest cheerleader

I encourage you to be your child's biggest fan, their cheer leader, and the one who supports them through all of the trials they will be facing.

Make sure they know that you're proud of them, and that you're there to help them. Use encouraging words and actions often. Let them know that you love them, and are there to support them no matter what.

Communicate regularly with their teachers

Keeping in good contact with your child's teacher is a great way to stay on top of problems before they arise. It will also help you keep track of any progress, or setbacks your child may be experiencing. It will also help you make sure your student is bringing home assignments, and not forgetting things at school.

If you homeschool, make sure to discuss your child with your spouse regularly, as well. That way you can work as a team to help them be more successful in daily endeavors.

Volunteer in the classroom

One of the best ways to see how your child is doing is to be present in their daily lives. If you can, I highly recommend volunteering in their classroom so you can see what your child's daily life is like. How they relate to others, and assess any areas that you might be able to help work on with your student.

Talk to your child

I know this may sound silly, but having a simple conversation daily with your child can do wonders for not only your relationship, but their sense of security as well. Discuss things like their friends, their schedule, their bus ride, what they did at lunch, recess time, and anything else they may be involved in. Find out how their day went, and any struggles they may have experienced.

Set goals

Set goals, both easy and more challenging, for your child. By keeping a chart of their goals, they can easily see any progress they're making which is a great motivator for them! Make sure to include some that will be easily attained to encourage them to move onto others that may be more of a challenge for them.

Get them involved

Get your child involved in extracurricular groups designed for special needs students where appropriate. If you homeschool, make sure to get your child engaged in activities outside the home such as special needs or homeschooling groups. This can help them develop emotional and social skills when dealing with others.

Here are a few excellent websites to help you get started.

- Autism Speaks
- Dianne Craft – Working with struggling learners
- Family Education – Homeschooling your special needs child
- Handwriting Without Tears - Program developed by an occupational therapist and handwriting specialist
- HSLDA Laureate Special Needs Software- Offers a variety of programs for language acquisition.
- List of National Organizations
- NATHHAN – National Challenged Homeschools Associated Network
- NHEN - Library of Special Needs Articles
- NorCal Center on Deafness, Inc - Offers workshops, social events, and a summer camp for the deaf and hard of hearing
- PACE– Special Needs Education
- Sensory Processing Disorder Foundation
- Special Needs Homeschooling

20

Getting Help

"Let the Word of Christ dwell in you richly, teaching and admonishing one another in all wisdom, singing psalms and hymns and spiritual songs, with thankfulness in your hearts to God." ~Colossians 3:16

Back when we decided to start a family not only excitement, but also overwhelming fear, struck right into me. It suddenly dawned on me that I had no clue what I was doing. And I don't know about you, but my babies didn't pop-out with an "Owner's Manual" that I could follow.

So what other option did I have but to cry out for help! I sought help from other mom's, tot groups, friends, and family. And eventually I came to Jesus. His Word teaches us exactly what we need to know to raise our children effectively.

As the years progressed and He placed homeschooling on my heart I again hit my wall of fear. Below is a conversation I had in response to that fear and I thought I would share it with you as well.

My prayer is that it will help and encourage you in your parenting journey. Today's taking action points are simply questions and answers that most parents have asked themselves at least once in their lives.

I hope that it helps you to gain some understanding into your calling as a parent, and into what God's will for your family is. I certainly don't know everything there is to raising children. Some days I don't feel like I know the first thing. But God does, and as long as I'm seeking wisdom from Him I can rest well.

"If any of you lacks wisdom, you should ask God, who gives generously to all without finding fault, and it will be given to you." James 1:5

My son, if you will receive my words and treasure my commandments within you, Make your ear attentive to wisdom, incline your heart to understanding; for if you cry for discernment, lift your voice for understanding; If you seek her as silver and search for her as for hidden treasures; Then you will discern the fear of the Lord and discover the knowledge of God. For the Lord gives wisdom; From His mouth come knowledge and understanding. ~ Proverbs 2:1-6

1. I'm scared.

The Lord himself goes before you and will be with you; he will never leave you nor forsake you. Do not be afraid; do not be discouraged. ~Deuteronomy 31:8

"And surely I am with you always, to the very end of the age." ~Matthew 28:20

2. I'm worried about what other people will think or say about myself or my children.

"Fear of man will prove to be a snare, but whoever trusts in the Lord is kept safe." ~Proverbs 29:25

"The fear of the Lord is the beginning of wisdom, and knowledge of the Holy One is understanding." ~Proverbs 9:10

"Set your mind on things above, not on things on the earth." ~Colossians 3:2

3. I doubt my own ability to raise my kids effectively.

"...for it is God who works in you to will and to act in order to fulfill his good purpose." ~Philippians 2:13

"I can do all things through Christ who strengthens me." ~Philippians 4:13

4. I don't think we can afford children.

"And God is able to bless you abundantly, so that in all things at all times, having all that you need, you will abound in every good work." ~2 Corinthians 9:8

5. How can I take care of my home, family, and daily responsibilities?

"If anyone serves, they should do so with the strength God provides, so that in all things God may be praised through Jesus Christ. To Him be the glory and the power for ever and ever. Amen." ~1 Peter 4:11

"And whatever you do in word or deed, do all in the name of the Lord Jesus, giving thanks to God the Father through Him." ~Colossians 3:17

6. I'm so overwhelmed; I don't even know where to start!

"Trust in the Lord with all your heart and lean not on your own understanding." ~Proverbs 3:5

"If any of you lacks wisdom, you should ask God, who gives generously to all without finding fault, and it will be given to you." ~James 1:5

"Be anxious for nothing, but in everything by prayer and supplication, with thanksgiving, let your requests be made known to God." ~Philippians 4:6

7. What about my free time?

"Do nothing out of selfish ambition or vain conceit. Rather, in humility value others above yourselves, not looking to your own interests but each of you to the interests of the others." -Philippians 2:3

"Come to me, all you who are weary and burdened, and I will give you rest." -Matthew 11:28

8. What if make a mistake?

"And do not be conformed to this world, but be transformed by the renewing of your mind, that you may prove what is that good and acceptable and perfect will of God." -Romans 12:2

9. What if others disapprove of our choices?

"But whatever were gains to me I now consider loss for the sake of Christ. What is more, I consider everything a loss because of the surpassing worth of knowing Christ Jesus my Lord, for whose sake I have lost all things." -Philippians 3:1-8

10. What about my attitude and, um...shall we say lack of patience?

"Do everything without grumbling or arguing, so that you may become blameless and pure, "children of God without fault in a warped and crooked generation". Then you will shine among them like stars in the sky as you hold firmly to the word of life. And then I will be able to boast on the day of Christ that I did not run or labor in vain. But even if I am being poured out like a drink offering on the sacrifice and service coming from your faith, I am glad and rejoice with all of you. So you too should be glad and rejoice with me." -Philippians 2:14-18

"Therefore, as God's chosen people, holy and dearly loved, clothe yourselves with compassion, kindness, humility, gentleness and patience." -Colossians 3:12

"...for the wrath of man does not produce the righteousness of God." -James 1:20

11. Um, so are you saying I'm going to be tested? Because we all know how that turns *out...*

"My brethren, count it all joy when you fall into various trials, knowing that the testing of your faith produces perseverance." -James 1:2-3

"And not only that, but we also glory in tribulations, knowing that tribulation produces perseverance; and perseverance, character; and character, hope. Now hope does not disappoint, because the love of God has been poured out in our hearts by the Holy Spirit who was given to us." -Romans 1:3-5

12. What if I can't hack it? I mean it's always easier said than done!

"...And let us run with perseverance the race marked out for us, fixing our eyes on Jesus, the pioneer and finisher of our faith. For the joy set before Him He endured the cross, scorning its shame, and sat down at the right hand of the throne of God. Consider Him who endured such opposition from sinners, so that you will not grow weary and lose heart." ~Hebrews 12: 1-3

13. How am I to raise my children?

I don't even have a child psychology degree! And they didn't exactly come with a "How-To Manual".

"These commandments that I give you today are to be on your hearts. Impress them on your children. Talk about them when you sit at home and when you walk along the road, when you lie down and when you get up. Tie them as symbols on your hands and bind them on your foreheads. Write them on the doorframes of your houses and on your gates." ~Deuteronomy 6-9

14. Okay, any final advice?

But He said to me, "My grace is sufficient for you, for my power is made perfect in weakness." Therefore I will boast all the more gladly about my weaknesses, so that Christ's power may rest on me. ~2 Corinthians 12:9

"He will feed his flock like a shepherd. He will carry the lambs in His arms, holding them close to His heart. He will gently lead the mother sheep with their young." ~Isaiah 40:11 NLT

And thus began our journey...

Trust His leading in everything you do, and you will be successful. Keep in mind that success will be defined by God, and not by man.

What is God calling your family to?
Where is He leading your children?

"...let us lay aside every weight, and the sin which so easily ensnares us, and let us run with endurance the race that is set before us, looking unto Jesus, the author and finisher of our faith..." ~ Hebrews 12:1-2

21

Why We Homeschool

"These commands that I give you today are to be on your hearts. Impress them on your children. Talk about them when you sit at home and when you walk along the road, when you lie down, and when you get up." - Deuteronomy 6:6-7

By now, most of you have figured out we are a homeschooling family. You may have found this book from my website, an online resource, or been referred to it by a friend.

We have homeschooled since the very beginning, so my children have never been in a public school setting.

Some of you might think we're crazy for homeschooling. Some might be concerned for the social well-being of our children. Some of you might even like the idea, and think we have it all together, and we've been confident in our choice to homeschool from the very beginning. But I assure you, it wasn't always that way.

Back before we started having children, we met a neighbor who homeschooled her children. I think the exact words that came out of my mouth following that meeting was "wow, I would NEVER!"

If you haven't already figured it out in your own lives, God has a sense of humor.

And a plan.

But sometimes that plan isn't quite in line with our plans.

But He has a way of convincing us to follow His will…

For example I swore up and down I would never marry a younger man. Did I mention that I'm 5 years older than my husband?

I swore I wouldn't marry someone from my own small home town. After all I was too good for that shabby little place. Ironically, my husband went to my same high school. I just didn't know it being 5 years older and all. His parents live about 10 minutes away from mine. And now that I'm older, I still consider Greeley my real 'home' even though I live an hour away.

I also swore I would never wear bell bottoms. I'll never forget the smile on my father's face the day I walked in with "flared" jeans on.

And under no circumstances would I ever be caught homeschooling. Or even think of quilting.

Yep, you' guessed it...I've done both. Actually, I still do both! Ironically, they're some of my favorite things now.

The only difference is that now I don't make bold statements like "I'll never"...anymore.

I'll never forget the day we met the most lovely homeschooling family. I knew my "I'll never" comment would come to bite me in the tush. The family was wonderful, and I wanted so much to be like them. I intently followed them around asking an obscene amount of questions, getting excited about curriculum, and hopeful that our family would soon look just like theirs.

After long discussions and prayer, we decided that we would homeschool. Once our oldest was old enough to keep her eyes open I started planning all kinds of educational activities for her and gearing up for preschool at home.

Yes, I was a tad over-enthusiastic.

But I was also afraid. I moved forward not with faith in our calling, but with a caveat...if it didn't go "well", we would put her in school. It was my 'get out of jail free card' if you will. We even started her a year early so worst case we could put her in a "real" school in the correct grade level with no harm done.

But God had other plans for our family. As each year passed, I continued with my "if it doesn't go well" mantra. But inevitably the year came when it didn't go so well. I had just had our third child, and frankly I was sick as a dog.

Homeschooling the other two was trying and there were many days when they did minimal school while I laid on the floor exhausted and nauseous. A little voice in my head repeated my motto from past years "You can just put them in school you know…"

My husband came home after a long day of cut and paste, cranky kids, failed crafts, and my oldest seemed to be behind in reading. Things weren't looking good. I casually mentioned to him that I was ready to put her in school. We could enroll her in 2nd grade and since she was a year ahead she should do well.

Up until that point my husband had also been a little wishy-washy about the whole homeschooling concept. But on that day God directed our path. Just before we were about to throw in our homeschooling towel, He stopped us.

My husband stepped up to the plate and confidently told me, "No, we are homeschooling."

He was confident that is what God called us to do, and neither of us wanted to be in disobedience to His will.

It wasn't until 3 years into our homeschooling journey, that I finally submitted to God's will for our family. I committed myself to the calling that He had for us and took a step out in faith.

And do you know what?

It was the absolute best year of homeschooling that we had. I didn't realize that previously my half-hearted approach was actually a detriment to my children's education.

For the first time I sat down and lesson planned, for real. I carefully chose curriculum, not that I hadn't done that prior, but this time it was with more of a long-term goal in mind. My husband helped choose our curriculum as well, which was a huge blessing to me.

Up until then I had mostly been in charge of our educational choices. And since I was also teaching our children, if things didn't go well, it all landed on me. Having my husband participate in our homeschooling choices on a more direct level lifted a huge weight off of my shoulders that I didn't even fully realize was there.

We moved forward from that point, and haven't looked back since.

Do I still doubt our choices? Yes, of course.

Just like other parents we doubt ourselves. And yes, we still have good days and bad days. But now we move forward with confidence and strength knowing that we are being obedient to God's calling in our life.

Homeschooling may not be for everyone, but it is what is best for our family.

I fully realize that homeschooling might not be on your radar right now. As I mentioned previously, I'm not trying to sell you on the concept. However I do want to point out that when taking charge of your child's education it's important to seek God's will regarding the matter.

If you've decided something contrary your struggle will be hard and your road long. So just take time when deciding your course of action. Pray fervently and listen closely to His answer for your family.

Oh, and just in case you were wondering, I didn't exactly get my wish to look like that other family.

We don't look anything like their family.

We look like our family.

And that's a beautiful thing in God's eyes.

Taking Action

There is no such thing as the perfect parent. My prayer is that after reading this book you would not feel condemned or like the worst parent on the planet. But instead that you will be inspired to make the necessary changes towards becoming the type of parent you want to be.

Raising children is not a temporary gig. It is truly a life long journey. But it is also one that is worth the effort. No matter how far along you are in your parenting journey, it's never too late to change!

So this final Taking Action task is to pray.

Pray for an open heart to be able to communicate with your child in a way that they will receive well.

Pray for a way to communicate effectively with your spouse and your children.

Pray for God's wisdom in decisions you're making for your family.

Pray for an open heart to receive whatever He is calling you to do.

Heavenly Father,

Thank you so much for the children you have entrusted to us. We come to you today seeking guidance, strength, and perseverance in our parenting journey. You are the perfect parent, and we seek to learn from Your example. Help us extend our children the same gentleness, grace, and mercy that you have showed towards us. Help us to raise them up in Your will, and lead them to You in all things. Please give them discernment between right and wrong, and help us to guide them in these choices. May they come to know you, and seek after you with their whole heart. We pray that our lives, and those of our children will be a living testimony and witness for Your glory. May our feet always walk in Your light, and our lives be pleasing to You.

Amen.

Things to remember...

"Commit to the Lord whatever you do, and he will establish your plans. ~ Proverbs 16:3

"And these words which I command you today shall be in your heart. You shall teach them diligently to your children, and shall talk of them when you sit in your house, when you walk by the way, when you lie down, and when you rise up. You shall bind them as a sign on your hand, and they shall be as frontlets between your eyes. You shall write them on the doorposts of your house and on your gates.

~ Deuteronomy 6:6-7

"For we are His workmanship, created in Christ Jesus for good works, which God prepared beforehand, that we should walk in them." - Ephesians 2:10

"Behold, children are a heritage from the Lord, the fruit of the womb a reward." - Psalms 127:3

"Train up a child in the way he should go; even when he is old he will not depart from it." - Proverbs 22:6

"And how from infancy you have known the Holy Scriptures, which are able to make you wise for salvation through faith in Christ Jesus. All Scripture is God-breathed and is useful for teaching, rebuking, correcting and training in righteousness, so that the man of God may be thoroughly equipped for every good work." ~ 2 Timothy 3:15-17

"Love is patient, love is kind. It does not envy, it does not boast, it is not proud. It does not dishonor others, it is not self-seeking, it is not easily angered, it keeps no record of wrongs. Love does not delight in evil but rejoices with the truth. It always protects, always trusts, always hopes, always perseveres. Love never fails." ~ 1 Corinthians 13:4-8a

---

"I have hidden Your Word in my heart that I might not sin against you." ~ Psalm 119:11

"In their hearts humans plan their course, but the Lord establishes their steps." ~ Proverbs 16:9

"His master replied, 'Well done, good and faithful servant! You have been faithful with a few things; I will put you in charge of many things. Come and share your master's happiness!" ~ Matthew 25:21

"Therefore, my beloved brothers, be steadfast, immovable, always abounding in the work of the Lord, knowing that in the Lord your labor is not in vain." ~ 1 Corinthians 15:58

"But all things should be done decently and in order." ~ 1 Corinthians 14:40

"Unless the Lord builds the house, its builder's labor in vain." ~Psalm 127:1

"But seek first His kingdom and His righteousness, and all these things will be given to you as well." ~Matthew 6:33

"Train a child in the way he should go, and when he is old he will not turn from it." ~Proverbs 22:6

"The fear of the Lord is the beginning of wisdom, and knowledge of the Holy One is understanding." ~Proverbs 9:10

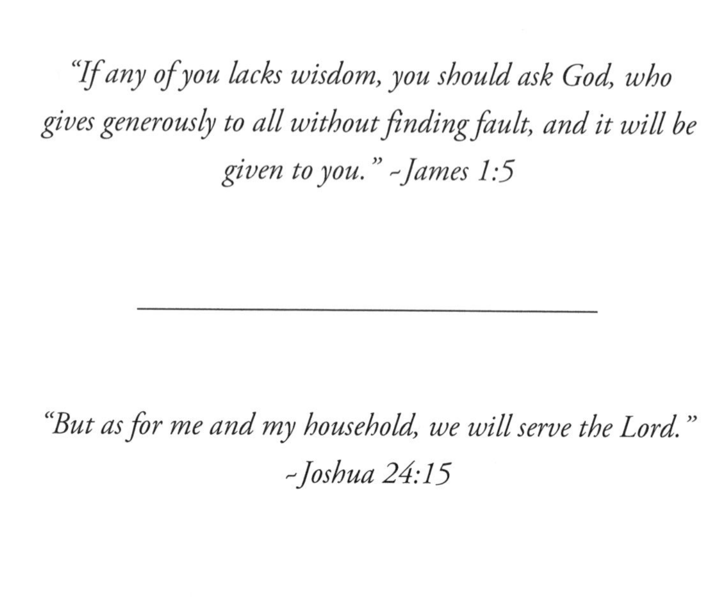

"If any of you lacks wisdom, you should ask God, who gives generously to all without finding fault, and it will be given to you." -James 1:5

"But as for me and my household, we will serve the Lord." -Joshua 24:15

"But as for you, continue in what you have learned and have firmly believed, knowing from whom you learned it and how from childhood you have been acquainted with the sacred writings, which are able to make you wise for salvation through faith in Christ Jesus." -2 Timothy 3:14-15 (ESV)

"If any of you lacks wisdom, you should ask God, who gives generously to all without finding fault, and it will be given to you." - James 1:5

"By wisdom a house is built, and by understanding it is established; by knowledge the rooms are filled with all rare and beautiful treasures." - Proverbs 24:3-4

"Let the Word of Christ dwell in you richly, teaching and admonishing one another in all wisdom, singing psalms and hymns and spiritual songs, with thankfulness in your hearts to God." - Colossians 3:16

"These commands that I give you today are to be on your hearts. Impress them on your children. Talk about them when you sit at home and when you walk along the road, when you lie down, and when you get up." ~ Deuteronomy 6:6-7

Erica Arndt is a Christian, a wife, a mom,
a homeschooler, and an author.
She is creator of the award winning website
www.ConfessionsofaHomeschooler.com,
and author of the top selling Homeschooling 101 book, a step
by step guide to getting started homeschooling.

Thank you!
To God for His many blessings,
my family for all of their support,
and to all of my loyal readers.
I hope this book blesses you and your family!

Visit Confessions of a Homeschooler

- Website: www.confessionsofahomeschooler.com
- Contact me: erica@confessionsofahomeschooler.com
- Facebook: facebook.com/ConfessionsofaHomeschooler
- Pinterest: pinterest.com/ericahomeschool
- Twitter: twitter.com/ericahomeschool
- YouTube: www.youtube.com/user/EricasHomeschool
- Instagram: instagram.com/ericaarndt

Interested in homeschooling, but don't know where to start?

Don't worry! Homeschooling 101 offers you a step by step practical guide that will help you get started and continue on in your homeschooling journey.

I will walk you through all of the steps to getting started, choosing and gathering curriculum, creating effective lesson plans, scheduling your day, organizing your home, staying the course, and more!

This book is a must read for new and prospective homeschoolers who need tangible advice for getting started!
It even includes helpful homeschool forms and a free planner!

Resources

- A New Wave of Evidence: The Impact of School, Family, and Community Connections on Student Achievement A. T. Henderson & K. L. Mapp. (Southwest Educational Development Laboratory, 2002)
- National Parent Teacher Association: www.pta.org
- National Education Association: www.nea.org
- Bible Verses are from www.biblegateway.com using the New International Version unless otherwise indicated.
- The Best Yes by Lysa Terkeurst

20013028R00108

Made in the USA
San Bernardino, CA
23 March 2015